DARE TO GO FROM F*CKED UP
TO FABULOUS

GRACE REDMAN

Foreword by Sunny Dawn Johnston

CAN I LIVE?!

Cover and Interior Design by
Transcendent Publishing
www.transcendentpublishing.com

TRANSCENDENT
publishing

Author Cover Photo and Headshots by
Hannah Lorsch Photo

ISBN: 979-8-9868507-1-9

Printed in the United States of America.

This book is dedicated to my mother, Abla Muhawieh Sahouria, to YOU, and to all the women in my life who have sacrificed so much of themselves to make the lives of others better. I SEE YOU! Today I want you to know YOU ARE WORTHY, NO MATTER WHAT, YOU are RESILIANT, YOU are a BADASS and YOU can CREATE a fabulous, delicious life you LOVE. Here's to the FREEDOM from your own inner mean girl! Cheers!

Out of suffering have emerged the strongest souls; the most massive characters are seared with scars.

–Khalil Gibran

Contents

Foreword

by Sunny Dawn Johnston

*M*ost of us have been in that place where we asked ourselves the very question Grace Redman poses. Whether consciously and direct, or silently within, the question, *Can I Live?* causes us to look at our past and brings us all together in a familiar way. When hard things happen, when loved ones die, when we've made choices that have caused pain, we ask ourselves: *Can I live through this? Can I live without them? Can I live with the consequences?*

What I LOVE about this beautiful book is that Grace takes it a step further. This book is not just about finding a way to live. It's about finding a way to LIVE the utterly fantastic life you were meant to live – not despite the pain – but just maybe, quite possibly, because of it.

What if each and every experience that you have had in your life has created the contrast within you that called you into seeking even greater light, greater love than you ever knew?

What if you aren't fucked up at all? What if you never were fucked up? What if the truth is, just as Grace shares so eloquently in this book, you were just repeating the patterns of your ancestors? The truth is, no one around you could tell you, let alone teach you that you weren't fucked up because of their own generational teachings and feelings of lack, worthiness, and self-love?

Of course, this isn't new information. Many of us know that this is true, but have you been able to really let go of those feelings deep within? Have you been able to tell that voice that tells you what you should have done or could have done better, to shut up? Have you been able to take your life back ... and live it in the most fabulous way you desire? If you have started down the path, but aren't quite there, this book will help!

In this book, Grace not only shares relatable stories from her life, but gives you concrete steps to move from Fucked up to Fabulous. She helps you find the courage to make lasting change by building up your awareness and understanding of why you do what you do. She gives you an honest peek inside her life and helps you to see how you can turn things around, just as she has done. That doesn't mean life is easy. It means you can live it on your terms, not the terms of those that came before you.

I have known Grace for over six years, and through those years, I have been honored to be a mentor to her as she has walked through some of the very challenges she shares in this book. One thing I can tell you about Grace ... she's real. If you are ready to truly look at your shit and begin the journey of healing, this book is going to open you up, help you to spit the old shit out, make you laugh out loud ... and ultimately, find the real YOU!

One thing that I absolutely LOVE and HONOR about Grace is her willingness to be vulnerable. The epilogue in this book is one of the most honest things I have read recently. We are always learning, growing, expanding, and healing, and it certainly isn't easy to share details of your life with the world ... AND Grace did it because she knows it will help others.

So, block some time off of your calendar, grab a notebook – cuz you are going to need it – and dig in. You will be so happy you did!

PS: Grace and I are both believers in the angels and the signs they bring. When she told me her publishing date was 11/11/22, I knew I had to write this foreword. It was 11 years ago, on 11/11/11, that I released my first book. Coincidence?? I think not

In Love, Light and Healing,
Sunny Dawn Johnston
Psychic Medium, Spiritual and Biz Mentor, Angel Expert & Author

Introduction

You, me, or nobody is gonna hit as hard as life. But it ain't about how hard ya hit. It's about how hard you can get hit and keep moving forward. How much you can take and keep moving forward. That's how winning is done.

–Rocky Balboa

I sat on the sidewalk, crying hysterically. The boy I was dating had just lost his temper over something trivial and exploded in a rage, grabbing my car keys from me as I tried to get away and throwing them onto the roof of a nearby office building. He then proceeded to punch me.

The physical pain was nothing compared to the shame, embarrassment, and disgust that radiated through my head, soul, and heart. The worst, though, was the paralyzing fear. I felt like laying down and never waking up again.

This was not a new situation. From my teens to my twenties, I consistently attracted abusive, toxic interactions – the result of lifelong low self-esteem. I simply didn't feel worthy of love, especially from males. Also, what I'd seen growing up – women in the world around me being emotionally and physically abused by the men in their lives – had no doubt contributed to this pattern within me.

I knew in my heart and soul that what I was experiencing was not normal (though many in my circle viewed it as such) but rather toxic and unhealthy. It also wasn't something I wanted to continue to accept. I wanted better for myself.

I started to pay more attention to my small inner voice, the one that whispered quietly to me that there was hope; that I could find a better way. Reflecting on those dark times, I now know it was God, Source, the Universe, our Higher Power – or whatever name you choose – who planted that hope and reason in my mind and pushed me to make a change.

The punch to the head from that boy was a catalyst for change. I couldn't reach out to anyone around me because that wasn't the way we did things in my circle. One didn't speak about emotional challenges; they just sucked it up, put on a happy face, and pretended all was perfect. Doing things any other way would be considered "social suicide."

Today, that lost, lonely teenage girl who was in such tremendous pain manages one of the most successful staffing firms in the San Francisco Bay Area. I'm also a certified Success and Transformation Coach, partnering with women to help them step into their highest and greatest potential, and I host a weekly podcast called *Real Talk with Grace Redman*. I am blessed to have a kind, respectful husband and two beautiful healthy sons. I've managed to heal many layers of my childhood trauma wounds and diminish my self-sabotaging behavior. It's taken time, commitment, resilience, determination, and consistency, plus a firm devotion to self-love and self-care, but it enabled me to manifest a fabulous life I LOVE!

I am honored and humbled to be able to share with you what I believe are the most important elements that helped me break generational cycles and rise from fucked up to fabulous.

In the moments following that punch to the head, I had an intuitive flash: I needed professional support and guidance. At nineteen I didn't have much money for a therapist, but through the grace of God I stumbled upon a Catholic Charities ad in a newspaper I was browsing through one day. They had a student therapy program and only charged eight dollars a session! I mustered up the courage and called them to make an appointment – the first of MANY.

When I first met Rebekah, a young therapist right out of school, neither one of us could have imagined it would be the beginning of a twenty-five-year relationship! I spent all these years working hard to overcome many challenges, including depression, anxiety, low self-esteem, codependency, a horrible body image and relationship with food, a need to people-please, and workaholism. I learned how to set boundaries, love myself, walk away from toxic situations, and most importantly, find my worth and step into my power! That incredible power that we all have inside of us.

In those early years in therapy although I felt alone, broken, and lost I had this deep drive and passion to better myself. I felt a strong hunger and desire to succeed. I am really not sure where that fire inside me to rise came from. Now as I think back, I believe it was the higher source we call God, The Universe, The Divine, The Creator, a Higher Power, Spirit. (Again, you can choose whatever feels right to you). God was always with me moving me through the darkness, giving me hope and visions of how amazing life could be.

I committed myself to therapy and to learn as much as possible about self-development and success and on I went pedal to the metal to be the best I could be. I did it. I succeeded at most everything I did, well probably because I chose things, I knew I would be good at and enjoyed doing. Although in my mind I never thought it was good enough, I wasn't good enough, I wasn't deserving or worthy. Nothing I did satisfied me. I never felt accomplished. I was constantly judging myself and still in patterns of perfectionism and I still worried so much about what people would think of me.

As a mother, wife, entrepreneur, homemaker, sister, friend, community member, employer, and colleague, I put tremendous pressure on myself. The constant efforting to be perfect had completely drained me, taken away my joy, and left me feeling empty and spent. Sometimes, I felt like laying down and falling asleep ... for good. There was a point where I blamed everything and everyone around me for my situation when, shit, there was no one to blame but myself. After all, I had created these ridiculous expectations, though, in my defense I'd done so unconsciously, based on my environment and my early life experiences.

I had spent years trying to live up to these ridiculous, self-sabotaging expectations. I not only ran a successful business, I also took care of all of the domestic responsibilities at home, including the cooking. I rarely ever said no to a request from a friend or family member who needed support or help; I was "room mom" at my children's school and made an effort to make it to all their games and school activities, and I was the master entertainer and hostess. Why? Because in the world I grew up in, that's what a "good woman" does. How was I self-sabotaging? Well, when we do so much just to prove we're good enough, we wind up depleting ourselves. Our innate human desire to feel worthy will never be quenched if we are expecting to gain our worth from anything outside of us. We will forever be on a hamster wheel, with nothing to show for it but disappointment.

While on that hamster wheel I was also, as mentioned earlier, constantly studying personal development and success, which made me the go-to person for my friends, family, and, eventually, my colleagues and clients. Given this, it wasn't that surprising when I was guided to take a wide range of self-mastery and coaching certifications; after all, I had been coaching others for years. Little did I know that stepping into the classroom would lead to my own transformation.

Right now you may be asking what I mean by "transformation." It is the transformation of healing and diminishing those wounds from my childhood; of letting go of the expectations, self-judgment, people-pleasing, and overdoing. It was the walking away from toxic situations and the reframing of limiting beliefs into empowering ones. It also meant owning my worth and stepping into my confidence, as well as the magic and fabulousness of creating a fun, abundant, amazing life. A life that I wake up to and am grateful for every day … even on the tough days.

I spent a lot of time in the dark, and let me tell you it was NOT fun; in fact, it really sucked. I want to help you to diminish that negative mental chatter in your head, help you stop being so hard on yourself, and teach you how to gain your self-worth so you can live that life you have been dreaming of – a life of fun, passion, peace, and joy. You don't have to be controlled by that mean girl in your head. You can choose to quiet her bitchy voice and raise the volume of the voice of the empowering, kind, loving woman who also lives within you.

Okay, I know what you are thinking! Really? How? First, you must make a decision. Are you ready to make a change? Are you ready to start loving yourself? I believe your answer is yes, or you wouldn't be reading this book. And, in saying yes, you have set the intention to make a powerful change in your life.

CONGRATULATIONS!!!

The critical voice in your head is typically related to your feelings of unworthiness – and the fears of not being good enough and of failing and looking stupid. You have created an unconscious story in your mind that you don't deserve joy, happiness, and abundance.

From the time we are born until the age of seven, we are in a type of hypnotic state; we are like sponges, absorbing everything we see and hear and creating stories based on that. We then live ninety-five percent of our lives from those unconscious (and usually false) stories and only five percent from a conscious state. WTF! REALLY??? Yes, Girl, really! Yeah, I know, that was my reaction too when I found out.

You are going to learn how to uncover those limiting beliefs hiding in your unconscious mind and reframe them into more empowering beliefs. These beliefs are what hold us back from living the lives we love; they are what make us worry about how we look to others; they put us in those states of stress and fear that drive us day in and day out. They trigger our childhood wounds and activate pain and stress in our bodies. You will learn how practicing self-love, forgiveness and gratitude, and committing to the universal laws, will help empower and transform you. Again, this is going to take commitment, con-sistency, determination and time. I can already hear you saying it: "I don't have the time." *Of course you do.* We all have the same twenty-four hours in the day, and I am confident that you have some "hidden" hours that are spent on what I call "waste-of-time" tasks; for example, spending too much time on Netflix or Tik Tok, gossiping on the phone, complaining to whoever will listen... the list can go on and on. Think about how those waste-of-time tasks are benefiting you. Okay, yes, sometimes we absolutely need them to unwind, but – let's be real – you probably need far less than you tell yourself.

If you are still reading, you ARE a courageous badass and ready to invest in yourself and in creating that fun and fabulous life you crave. The magic about committing to and taking action toward cultivating this life is that, as you begin to transform and elevate, you energetically help those around you shift as well. It is an amazing phenomenon I never believed until I experienced it. They will be looking to you as a mentor and a role model of what is possible.

I didn't always believe that we have choices; I for sure didn't believe we have everything we need inside us, because I was always looking outside myself for answers and validation. I have been in situations where I felt hopeless and powerless. Knowing what I know now, I understand that I always had a choice – even if it was to find the gratitude in a shitty situation. You too have choices. You can either stay stuck in the sticky, annoying black tar, or you can join me on an adventure, learning how to create that fun and fabulous life you dream of – and inspire others to do the same!

There was a time when I took a break from my sessions with Rebekah because I was in a really good place. Then shit would crop up again like a stubborn weed because I fell back into my people-pleasing habits and was having trouble setting boundaries with difficult personalities. Before I knew it, I was back in Rebekah's office dealing with the same toxic situations. In true Rebekah style, she immediately called me out on my shit, namely, my attachment to staying stuck in that sticky black tar. I'll never forget the day she shot me this really annoyed look and said, "You know what, Grace? Please, just go home. I don't even know what to tell you. You have been coming into my office for twenty years and it's the same story. I need to really think about how to approach this with you." I was like, *Damn, okay,* and I left.

When I went back the following week. she told me I had a hard choice to make: I could either save myself, my husband, and my kids, or I could keep worrying about what everyone else thought of me and die like my mother under the stress of toxicity and dysfunction. And she was right: it was a hard choice – one of the hardest of my life – yet, in that moment, I made it.

I chose myself and my family. I made a decision to set boundaries and let go of situations that didn't serve me. It was that moment that catapulted me to begin the very difficult deep healing process to get me to the place of freedom I enjoy today. I am not going to front, it was a long, painful journey, but the breakthroughs I experienced when I allowed myself to take the deep dive into my darkness and pain were absolutely priceless. They say that the deeper the pain you experience, the greater the ecstasy on the other side of that pain. I believe that to be true.

Rebekah retired several years ago, and as we sat in our last session together, she made a rather surprising admission: the first day we met she'd believed there was no hope for me. She felt I would continue to walk down the same path of abuse, low self-esteem, depression, and anxiety, just like the generations before me. She profusely apologized for thinking this way, saying she was a novice at that time and didn't know any better.

I wasn't offended at all by Rebekah's words. In fact, I felt a tremendous sense of accomplishment. I had broken many unhealthy cycles and manifested and created an incredible life. Granted, it WAS NOT easy, but I did it and you can too!

There is one question I want you to think about right now. Can you imagine yourself in one, two, or five years from now in the same place you are today? The answer is probably a HELL NO! I am so excited and honored you are here with me, and I promise I've got your back. It isn't going to be a walk in the park because digging deep, being honest with yourself, and making changes can be a bitch, but I promise the results will be so worth it. Now that you have made a commitment to yourself you have launched what Abraham-Hicks refers to as your "rockets of desire" into the Universe to help guide you toward your dreams. You are brave enough; you have done hard things before and you can do this too.

In the pages ahead, I will share my own personal experiences, as well as what helped me transform my life. All I ask is that you take what feels right to you and leave the rest.

Let's do this!

Chapter One

The Secret Sauce: Love Yourself!
You Are Fabulous!

Self-Love is the greatest middle finger of all times.
–Unknown

There I sat on the doctor's table, bawling my eyes out. My body felt very weak, like I was carrying a ton of bricks on my shoulders, and my chest was so heavy I could barely breathe. Truly, I don't know how I even made it to the appointment that day. I had a toddler and newborn baby, a husband, extended family, and my business staff relying on me. Plus, my mother had recently died at the age of fifty, and as the oldest daughter I was expected to "step up" and take care of the family – this, in addition to all my other responsibilities, and with very little, if any, support. The pressure was unbearable, which was how I ended up a complete hot mess in the office of a doctor I didn't even know. He was such a kind, gentle, and loving soul, and provided exactly what I needed at that moment: someone to validate me, someone to tell me that it was going to be okay, someone to just listen to me without judgment, criticism, or defensiveness. In my mind, I was a failure; I was weak. Only weak people cried and couldn't handle the load. That was the message that played like a loop: *Suck it up, Grace! What is wrong with you?! Don't cry, you got this! Just get up and go!* As I think back on that day, I feel such a sense of compassion for that young version of me. Had

I had a strong sense of self-love at that time, I may have saved myself a lot of severe mental and physical anguish.

The gracious and gentle doctor told me that I needed to take care of myself. That I wouldn't be able to help and support any of the people who relied on me if I didn't take care of myself first. We women are nurturing and loving beings; we feel a tremendous sense of joy and fulfillment when we give to others. Where we go wrong is putting everyone else first all of the time until we have nothing for ourselves. There is a reason when you get on a flight that the person making the public service announcement tells you to please put your oxygen mask on first. You wouldn't drive your car on an empty tank, would you? Even your car needs regular maintenance or it will break down on you, yet we continue to go, go, go and give, give, give until our own cup is empty. And, my lovely friend, you cannot give from an empty cup. You can only give from a cup that is overflowing. I have come to understand this, and that self-love and self-care are synonymous; I rarely feel selfish or guilty for taking care of ME. But let me tell you, sister, it has taken a lot of hard work and deep digging to get to this point!

I'd always had a need to people-please, to be liked, and to be perfect; I had always taken on too much, was afraid to say no, and didn't set strong boundaries. These patterns, now coupled with suppressed grief over losing my mother, had set me on the course toward a breakdown. It took me a while to realize that recovering from burnout takes so much more time and energy than it does to consistently practice self-love. Trust me, avoid the crash by making caring for yourself a daily habit; you will not regret it.

There are so many ways you can practice self-love, and we will touch on some of those ways later in the book. For now, I am going to talk about a few key practices that I have found integral to this work.

1. Release the need to people-please

2. Set your boundaries

3. Learn to say no

4. Don't listen to the critics

5. Honor all of your emotions

6. Rest. Rest. Rest.

The reason we people-pleasers typically have a hard time setting boundaries and saying no is fear. We are afraid that we will upset someone, afraid we may look like the "bad" person, afraid we won't be accepted if we don't do what the person asks.

I am just going to be real: not everyone is going to like you and that's okay! There are also going to be people in your life who, no matter what you do for them and how far out of your way you go for them, will never be happy or satisfied. Just accept that NOW. I know, because I have been there. You are thinking, *If I try hard, if I give more, if I act better, they will see how good I am and will value and accept me.* Um, yeah, NO, they will not! And here is a fabulous empowering TRUTH: you are worthy, no matter what those people think.

As I mentioned earlier, we usually fall into people-pleasing behavior because somewhere in our childhood we learned that if we pleased others we would be rewarded with praise or other types of attention. There isn't anything wrong with wanting to help or give to others; as humans we are wired to connect, to serve, to help each other. That said, we get out of alignment when we give or help with the intention of getting something in return, and that something is validation, affection, and acceptance. Well, as the saying goes, expectations are planned disappointments.

> Disclaimer: We typically get triggered and angry when a person doesn't meet our rules and expectations yet, in reality, they have no idea about our rules and expectations. And vice-versa, people get triggered and angry with us when we don't meet their rules and expectations and, again, most of the time we have no idea about their rules and expectations. This is the main reason that communication is vital in all of our interactions. People can't read our mind and we can't read their minds. Please be aware that communication is GOLDEN.

However, when we love ourselves, when we know our worth, we don't feel the need to please others; rather, we give because we want to. We give from a place of love – for others and for self – we get back love in return.

Now that you understand the reason behind your people-pleasing and the need to release it, I invite you to begin practicing self-love with those you can't please by setting boundaries with them. It is the best way to put distance between yourself and a draining or toxic situation.

To be real, if you are feeling that the relationship is out of whack, it's likely that way for the other person as well. Here is another harsh truth for those of us who over-give or are too nice: other people's emotions are *not* our responsibility. To be clear, this doesn't mean we can do whatever we want without regard for others. It means that if we set a boundary and the person gets upset, it's not our problem. They are responsible for how they choose to manage their emotions. Fuck … that's a tough one to accept, but it's so true.

This is a good place to talk about "unconditional love," a term I have struggled with. Early on, I believed it meant you were there for the person NO MATTER WHAT. But that felt off to me, especially when I was caught up in toxic situations. Putting up with whatever a person dishes out isn't healthy at all!

Unconditional love isn't about being manipulative (i.e., "I am only going to love you as long as you do this for me,") nor is it about being a doormat.

Unconditional love is all about accepting people for who they are and where they are on their journey. You can be in a relationship for many years and naturally outgrow the person but *still* love them unconditionally. Hell, you can love someone unconditionally and not even like them. I'm sure we've all got a few examples of that one in our lives! You can also love someone unconditionally from a distance, or even choose not to have them in your life.

Perfecting the art of unconditional love starts with *you*. When we lean into our imperfections and accept and love ourselves just the way we are, we begin to see the beauty in the imperfections of others. It then becomes so much easier to love without conditions and expectations. Again, this doesn't mean that we have to stay friends or have these toxic people in our lives; it just means releasing the anger and moving into a place of love. I am not in any way, shape, or form suggesting that you don't feel into your anger. It's important to honor the full range of your emotions, as they all serve a purpose in our healing. By the same token, if you aren't in a space to feel love in a certain situation, don't push yourself. Hey, sometimes we need to acknowledge where we are (in other words, not be phony with the "love and light" if we aren't feeling it).

Everything in our lives is a reflection of how we love ourselves. When you show yourself love and support by setting boundaries, you will attract people who love you in the same way. And, since energy attracts like energy, once you experience how good that feels you will get better and better at setting the boundaries, and better and better at attracting people who value you into your life.

Love yourself enough to set boundaries. Your time and energy are precious. You get to choose how you use it. You teach people how to treat you by deciding what you will and won't accept.

–Anna Taylor

We teach people how to treat us; that's essentially what we're doing when we set boundaries. Hand in hand with that is learning that "no" is a complete sentence. I used to have such a hard time saying no, my chest would tighten with dread any time I knew I had to. During the course of my journey, I came to understand the importance of saying the word no – in fact, it is one of the most powerful self-love tools we have.

We have a hard time saying "no" for some of the same reasons we have a hard time setting boundaries – i.e., not wanting to be considered a bad person and wanting to be loved and accepted. However, when we don't say no, we take on too much, get stretched too thin, and become overwhelmed and frustrated. We also become resentful of what we "have" to do and the person asking for it. When you say yes when you want to say no, the energy behind your "yes" isn't sincere; you are not being true to yourself. Also, the person will be able to pick up on that resentful energy, and that doesn't feel good to them either. Of course, there will be exceptions, for example, if your friend wants to go to a restaurant you aren't crazy about but you say yes. This is where gratitude comes in. You say yes because you value your relationship and you're grateful for the opportunity to spend time with someone you love and have fun with.

When someone asks you for something and you simply don't have the bandwidth, be transparent, letting them know in a kind, gentle, and firm way that you would love to help but you have a full plate at this time. You can also, *if you mean it*, tell them to reach out again in the future. Then again, while I believe transparency is important, I also believe you have every right to pick and choose how much you share and with whom. Remember, no is a complete sentence, meaning you can say it without further explanation. With practice, saying no will become easier, and when you do say yes, you will do so freely and with joy.

Now, I would not be doing my job if I did not prepare you for the major resistance, you will likely encounter when you release your people-pleasing behavior, learn to set boundaries, and start saying no. The people in your life may begin criticizing you, calling you crazy, and going on about how you have changed. Your response: "Yes, I have changed! I have taken my power back and WHAT YOU GONNA DO 'BOUT THAT?!" In time, those people will get with the program or distance themselves, and those who are more loving and supportive will step in. I am sure you can think of times in your life when that has already happened. That, my friends, is one of the laws of the Universe, and the laws of the Universe are very magical and clever. It is an energy game and like attracts like.

The most empowered person in the room is the person who is neutral and takes nothing personally.

–Grace Redman

Other people may criticize and talk shit behind your back. This is tough to swallow, but the truth is, it's really none of your business. I know, easier said than done, but think about it – if you are solid in your self-love and your worth is locked down tight, why would what others say bother you? When we are vulnerable, we begin to believe what others say about us. When we love ourselves, we understand that their opinions have nothing to do with us and have everything to do with their own insecurities, based on their own life imprints and experiences.

In fact, getting curious about others helped me stop taking their behavior and their words personally. More often than not, we have no idea what is going on in another person's life. Now, this does not excuse poor behavior – we still get to set boundaries – but placing the focus on them helps release us from internalizing their aggression and turning it on ourselves. You realize that the person you thought was ignoring you wasn't ignoring you at all; they were just going through a very rough time and they didn't have the bandwidth to give anything to anyone.

Just as you cannot stand in your worth, confidence, and self-love when you are constantly listening to others, you cannot do so when you're listening to your own negative mind chatter. The wonderful thing is that while you can't completely shut off your mind, you can change that mean girl asshole voice in your head to one that is more loving and more compassionate.

How do we do this? By replacing negative thoughts with positive ones. Would you ever talk to a five-year-old girl the way you talk to yourself (i.e., that you are a failure or stupid)? No, you wouldn't. The next time that negative mean voice starts talking, imagine it is talking to your five-year-old self and change it accordingly. Remember, you have complete control of the tracks that play in your mind. You can change the channel!

Self-Love is not selfish; you can't truly love another until you know how to love yourself.

–Unknown

A key factor of self-love is giving yourself permission to feel all of your emotions. As women, we are told by society that if we express our anger, frustration, or any other negative emotion, we are difficult, a bitch, a nagger. That is the furthest from the truth. It is an absolute must for us to express and feel our anger and any other emotion that comes up. Giving ourselves permission to feel and express what we feel is necessary! It is self-love. There is no reward for being a "nice" martyr and internalizing your emotions.

When we are unapologetic about taking care of ourselves, we inspire others to do the same. Knowing your value, loving yourself, and believing in yourself independent of what others think of you is powerful and contagious! It is also powerful when you take responsibility for your life because no one else is going to do it for you. Others can only love you and support you to the degree that you love and support yourself. We live in a country and in a time that has the most resources and the most opportunities for women, and it is up to us to leverage those opportunities by loving ourselves and stepping into our highest and greatest God given potential.

Also, by practicing self-love on a daily basis you will feel stronger, more grounded, and more empowered to respond to the inevitable challenges that are necessary for your growth. Each day we have a choice on how to meet those challenges and adversities.

I don't want to leave out an important factor of self-love and that is rest. Rest is so underrated. We take pride in going pedal to the metal. We take pride in sleepless nights and working long hours. We wear our grind like a badge of honor. What I want to emphasize is that rest is essential to our ability to meet our challenges. We can't meet our challenges and thrive if we are burned out and not taking the time to rest and do nothing. I give you permission to rest! Rest rejuvenates us and often-times provides us with the clarity we need to identify solutions to our challenges.

I speak from experience. Today, twenty years after sitting in the doctor's office, I am a completely transformed woman. Sometimes I can't even believe how far I have come in rewriting the bullshit stories that put me in that office. My life isn't perfect, but I can tell you I consistently experience joy, fun, fabulousness, freedom, peace, and abundance beyond my wildest dreams, and I know there is more to come.

When we make the relationship with ourselves and our Creator our main priority, our relationships with others become much easier. When we accept and own that we were created in the image of our Creator, we know that we are worthy no matter what. Releasing the people-pleasing, setting boundaries, saying no, and changing the channel on the mean girl voice will move us into the beautiful and magical state of self-love. When we love ourselves, we radiate a love that touches each and every person we interact with. And I KNOW that impacting the lives of others and making a difference in our world is very important to you, and, my beautiful friend, that change starts with you.

Activity

I invite you to set aside at least 15-30 minutes for this exercise. Go to a quiet place where you feel comfortable and, if possible, light a candle. Grab your journal, then allow your memory to guide you back to a time in your life when you were very hard on yourself. Now I want you to write a letter to that younger version of yourself using the same loving, compassionate words you would offer your best friend. Reread the letter to yourself each morning over the next five days. This is an extremely powerful way to heal and move on from painful memories that may be keeping you stuck.

Chapter Two

Get Addicted to Gratitude!

Gratitude is a powerful process for shifting your energy and bringing more of what you want into your life. Be grateful for what you already have and you will attract more good things.
–Rhonda Byrne, author of *The Secret*

To this day I am curious as to why it took so long for the true magic of gratitude to enter my life. I had been studying self-development since the age of fifteen, yet for some odd reason I wasn't ready to hear about and accept the practice of gratitude until I was in my early forties. I am certain it was mentioned in all the books I read, and that if I had learned and incorporated its practice earlier, I would have saved myself so much hustle. Instead, I was unconsciously focusing on lack as a way to motivate me to achieve and accomplish my goals and desires. It was a story I created and my ego was holding onto it for survival. Because this belief was so tied to my identity, it took a long time to shift the story from an energy of lack and hustle to an energy of gratefulness, both for what I already had and what was to come.

The only reason we want something is that we believe it will make us feel better, that it will bring us happiness, freedom, or security. Be grateful for the things you already have and you will open the door to feeling better. What a concept – and one that made no sense to me for a long time. Hey, at times I can be a slow and stubborn student! I am urging you to not make the same mistake I did. Start stepping into your gratitude and you will see the magic unfold quickly.

Each day, acknowledge and appreciate your accomplishments, even the small ones. Great accomplishments are rarely created overnight; they are usually built on years of tiny steps forward. Gratitude is key to helping you attract more of what you want. When we are operating from a place of stress and not allowing time to celebrate and appreciate what we are creating along the way, it takes us longer and we have to work much harder.

I want to share with you something I learned from my cousin and colleague, Diana Allen. It's called the Celebration Mindset and it's about celebrating and being grateful for your failures because those failures are helping you gather information and learn what you really want. I don't believe in failure, only feedback, so this concept she shared really resonated.

The dark side and shadow of gratitude, appreciation, and thankfulness are lack, not enough, and not good enough. Most often our negative thoughts of lack have become a habit; we have simply had the same thought so many times that they are now automatically predominant.

When we are caught in the cycle of lack, we will perpetuate more lack into our lives. Sure, we can grind and hustle to get what we want, but the underlying motivator is fear. Fear exhausts us and steals our joy. We put in motion a very different type of energy when we are taking action from a place of gratitude, appreciation, and thankfulness. You cannot be in fear and in gratitude at the same time. Of course, fear absolutely has its benefits. If you are in the forest and see a big black bear you better pray your FEAR kicks in so you know to RUN. Fear is a natural emotion that the human species needed to survive as cavemen when we had to run from wild animals and protect our lives. These days, however, thanks to the natural evolution, growth, and expansion of the human race, most fear is irrational. I really can relate to this acronym: False. Evidence. Appearing. Real.

No matter what we are going through and what we are experiencing there is always abundance surrounding us. There is always something to be grateful for.

When we begin to consistently practice gratitude, we naturally get closer to our true selves and to our higher power. We vibrate higher, and when we vibrate higher, we open ourselves up to opportunities we never imagined possible. It goes hand-in-hand with self-love. When we practice gratitude, our cup will begin to get full and eventually overflow. We will begin to have more energy, and when we have more energy there is more of us to share so we can make a difference for others and for ourselves.

Practicing gratitude brings you back into alignment instead of being so exhausted from focusing on everything that isn't going well and the heartache that comes with that. As Allan Lokos, author and founder of The Community Meditation Center, said, "Suffering usually relates to wanting things to be different than they are."

Many of us spend so much time wishing for things to be better or wondering what's next that it's really easy to over-look the blessings that are right in front of us. Now, being grateful for what is right in front of us, even if it isn't ideal, doesn't mean we are settling. It means we appreciate the experience in the moment and are eager and open to more and better. Once we begin to appreciate and be grateful for what we already have, we attract more love, joy, happiness, health, and wealth into our lives.

The Struggle Ends Where Gratitude Begins.

–Neale Donald Walsh

I'm going to show you why practicing an attitude of gratitude is the real secret to achieving your desires and creating a life of abundance.

When was the last time you thanked your partner, spouse, child, or friend for something they did for you? Maybe you can't even remember. On the other hand, do you find yourself constantly nagging them about all the things they got wrong? Start to show gratitude to those around you for the things that go well and watch the magic happen. They'll feel great, you'll feel great, and your life will be all the richer for it.

Be grateful for the challenging moments in your life as well. These are opportunities to grow through valuable life lessons. Remaining grateful through trying times not only builds re-silience, it also strengthens your faith.

In his book, *Think Like a Success, Act Like a Success*, Steve Harvey illustrates this point when he says even a homeless man living under the bridge has something to be grateful for. The cardboard box and the bridge he takes shelter under shield him from the wind and cold.

I recommend following these steps to cultivate your attitude of gratitude:

1. Address the mental chatter: there is a definite relationship between our thoughts and our moods. Think about all of the things you're grateful for in your life right now. Try to feel negativity while you're thinking about these things. I bet you can't do it. Thinking thoughts of gratitude leaves no room for pessimism or self-sabotage.

2. Train your mind: start small by zipping your lip when you're about to complain. I know it's hard and there are always going to be days you feel like cursing everyone to you-know-where, but that's okay. The next hour is a new hour and tomorrow is a new day.

3. Tune in: while you are going through your day, be aware of what's around you. Reflect on those everyday moments, from the smile your child throws you as he's leaving for school to the cup of coffee your spouse pours for you as you rush around the kitchen packing lunches. You will soon discover you have so much more to be grateful for than you realized.

Every adversity, every failure, and every heartache carries with it the seed of an equivalent greater benefit.

–Napoleon Hill

Everyone goes through dark and difficult times. They are an inevitable part of life. But how we deal with them – and most importantly what we learn – is key to moving forward and getting back on track.

When you're in the midst of a deep, dark storm the most natural thing to come to mind is to ask why. *Why is this happening to me?!* I get it. That's exactly what I've done when faced with difficulties.

But as I've moved forward in this adventure called life, I reflected and came to understand why certain things happened the way they did. It was all for a greater purpose. The ugly messy times helped me to grow and better prepare for the next storm. I've realized that each situation I face is just a stepping-stone to a greater expanded experience, if I allow it to be so. If I don't allow it, and learn from the experience, I will continue to be faced with similar challenging situations.

Difficult times can actually benefit us. Adverse situations can teach us so much.

They:

- build our character
- deepen our understanding of ourselves
- teach us how to cope
- up our resilience and wisdom stores
- grow our compassion levels, helping us to help others during their hard times
- enable us to realize the darkness doesn't last forever and the light will eventually shine again

Take a minute now to think back to some of your most challenging times. Can you find the gratitude in those moments? Can you see the greater good that came from it? What did you learn? Did your life perspective change? I bet the answer is a big, "Hell YES!"

Pain is a part of life and without it, we'd struggle to truly appreciate pleasure and joy. So when pain next hits, remember this: it's up to you to decide whether you allow it to define, destroy, or strengthen you.

It really all comes down to your mindset. Staying in the down days for too long can be detrimental. Our thoughts absolutely change our reality. You need to find something to be thankful for to help you get out of the rut. And there is ALWAYS something to be thankful for.

To illustrate, here's a story from my life:

My mother was only fifty years old when she lost her battle with cancer. It was devastating. At that time, I just couldn't see the positive in the situation. But after some time of grieving and pain, I began to reflect on the moment of her passing and I saw it in a new light.

She passed in the comfort of her home surrounded by family and friends. She wasn't left alone for one single moment as we all took turns sitting with her even though, at times, it was really crowded! It was a house full of love and I know she felt the love as her soul was preparing to make the transition out of her body. And that is my something to be thankful for in a very devasting situation.

From that experience, I also learned that finding a positive in the negative is a leadership attribute. I've made sure to keep that in mind when I'm helping others deal with their hard times.

The more you praise and celebrate your life, the more there is in life to celebrate.

–Oprah Winfrey

Now, I'm not naive enough to think everyone will always find a happy ending. But I do know that at the very least, a dark time will always teach us a lesson, be it big or small. What so many of us learned from my mom was to live life to the fullest because you never know what's around the corner. Oh, and don't sweat the small stuff, girl! I was also grateful to learn these lessons from her.

If you're going through a difficult time and having a hard time feeling gratitude, I hope these words have helped in some way. What is something you can be grateful for today?

Your mind travels down the road you set it to. If you set the GPS in your mind to frustrated, angry, sad, and resentful, then your mind will take you on a nasty ride to that very destination. But if you set it to a place filled with gratitude, fun, and happiness, you'll enjoy a relaxed and peaceful joyride. Here is something I went through recently that really brought home to me how resilient our minds are.

I had my GPS set firmly on joy, gratitude, and happiness. I spent time with family and friends I hadn't seen in a while and cooked up a storm with my boys. We ate tons of mouth-watering food and spent time relaxing in the sun, listening to amazing music.

But even after a fabulous week, the princess of darkness still managed to rear her ugly head and take me on a "woe-is-me" ride. Just what brought the princess of darkness pounding on my door? It was a casual slip of the tongue.

While speaking with a friend, I was reminded of the tremendous pain and hurt someone had inflicted on me years earlier. Right away, my mind went on a journey back to a time when I felt devastated, hurt, alone, and abandoned.

Now, in the present moment, I wasn't any of those things. On the contrary, I was in a great place, surrounded by love and support. But the pain I felt from that past experience came rushing over me like a tidal wave. I felt a deep sense of darkness and sadness. I just kept running the situation in my mind like a horror movie, getting more upset and resentful by the minute. And I wallowed in that sadness for a couple of days. I ate more than enough See's Candy and did everything in slow motion. I felt TERRIBLE.

By taking myself to that past devastating experience, I was allowing my mind to live it all over again. Our mind doesn't know the difference between *then* and *now*. It just knows what we are focusing on in the moment! Duh, Grace, light bulb moment.

And then another thought hit me: "Wait, don't I teach this?" So I resolved to practice what I preach and redirected my focus to what I was grateful for *now*. I also remembered that I wouldn't be who I am today if I didn't have that bad experience. That painful experience helps me help others when they're experiencing difficult times.

To shift my state and help myself get back into alignment, I put on my favorite playlist, called my bestie, and hit the gym. Within a couple of days, I had gone from a deep, dark place to feeling myself again all thanks to gratitude and focusing on all the blessings I have in my life right now.

Gratitude is a very powerful practice. It turns not enough into enough and – again, per the magical Law of Attraction – it brings more amazing things and experiences into our lives.

Now, why the hell wouldn't we want to practice gratitude when it will only bring us what we want and open the flood-gates to more?

My life changed DRAMATICALLY when I learned the concept of gratitude and began shifting my mindset from focusing on everything that sucked to focusing on what was good now. I am very blessed and privileged to own a very suc-cessful staffing business that has consistently provided generous revenues. However, during the 2009 economic downturn I woke up and found my business was pretty much "gone" (our billings had gone from thousands a week to almost nothing.) It was, aside from the Great Depression, one of the worst downturns in US history, setting off ripples of fear and panic across the country. For me, the devastation was all-en-compassing. Not only did it provide my livelihood, but at that time I had tied myself worth to my production and income, so you can imagine the hit my ego took. Sure, it was a "first-world" problem, but in that moment, I was consumed with pain, the feeling of failure, and fear!

I did sit in my fear for a while, then, knowing that wasn't serving myself, my family, or my business, I made the com-mitment to shift my mindset. I had read many stories of people who were very successful during dire economic times, and I turned to them now for guidance. What propelled them to succeed during those challenging times was their mindset and their focus on gratitude and what was going well, instead of everything that wasn't.

Gratitude is the healthiest of all human emotions. The more you express gratitude for what you have, the more likely you will have even more to express gratitude for.

–Zig Ziglar

I decided to challenge myself, pull myself out of my pity and start focusing on all the blessings in my life at that time: my beautiful and healthy children, my supportive and loving husband, my health, the amazing friends we had, the incredible privilege of serving the community, the success we had experienced … my list went on and on.

At the end of the year, though our profits were not as robust as in previous years, we still came out ahead when most other staffing firms had closed their doors.

There have been many scientific studies conducted on the habit of practicing gratitude and how it improves our mental health, physical health, our confidence, our relationships, and our over-all outlook on life. An article titled, *Expanding the Science and Practice of Gratitude*, published by the Greater Good Science Center at UC Berkeley, noted that gratitude has a lasting effect on the brain and may contribute to improved mental health over time. Just like the thoughts of lack have become a habit, it will take time to instill the habit of gratitude in your mind, so commit to a daily practice and be patient with yourself.

In an article for NBC Today Show, Laura Dunn included the following quote from UC Davis psychology professor Robert A. Emmons: "Clinical trials indicate that the practice of gratitude can have dramatic and lasting effects in a person's life. It can lower blood pressure, improve immune function and facilitate more efficient sleep."

A recent study from the University of California San Diego's School of Medicine found that people who were more grateful actually had better heart health:

"They showed a better well-being, a less depressed mood, less fatigue and they slept better," said the study's author, Paul J. Mills. "When I am more grateful, I feel more connected with myself and with my environment. That's the opposite of what stress does."

Given the existing body of scientific evidence – and the on-going research yielding positive results – what is stopping you from committing to practicing gratitude?

Set aside time each day to become aware of and address your negative mental chatter and write down what you are grateful for now and you will absolutely experience a shift in your days. At first, it may show up as a happier mood and outlook, followed by new or improved good experiences and relationships.

Gratitude Exercise

I invite you to think back on some of the challenging moments in your life. Pick one of those moments and take some time to get quiet and reflect. What are three gratitudes that you can take away from that challenging time? What lesson did you learn that helped you grow as a person and gain wisdom?

Chapter Three

Are You Drinking the Poison?

Today I decided to forgive you. Not because you apologized, or because you acknowledged the pain you caused me, but because my soul deserves peace.

–Najwa Zebian

"Forgive and forget? I am neither Jesus nor do I have Alzheimer's!" That was the saying on a Kermit the Frog meme that I used as the picture for my forgiveness blog. Can I tell you that blog received thousands of shares that spanned across the country? Why?? Because forgiveness can be so challenging and that line, though funny, really resonated with so many.

Like me and Kermit, your first reaction when you hear the word forgiveness probably goes something along the lines of, "What do you mean, just forgive? How can I? That person did me wrong and you want me to forgive just like that? Hell no! I want my justice!"

There have been times when forgiving is the last thing I wanted to do. In fact, just thinking about forgiving made my blood boil and I felt like punching the wall!

Little hurts or betrayals that we sweep under the rug multiply. It's like a coffee cup we just rinsed out without washing – the layers of coffee become dark and stain the cup. When we keep sweeping our hurts under that rug, they can stain our hearts. Our heart doesn't get stained because we are a bad or dark person. It gets stained and hardened as a way for us to protect ourselves. What we don't realize is that when we close off our hearts out of fear, we are also closing it to love. I have seen this so many times with my clients and, frankly, I have also done it myself. When we get hurt and sit in unforgiveness, we unconsciously hold the aggression against loved ones who *haven't* betrayed us. We think that because we were hurt once it is going to happen again and we don't allow ourselves to fully be present in our relationships.

I totally get it! I thought that forgiving the betrayal was like saying it was okay, and there was no part of me that was ready to do that. Just thinking about it created anxiety and tremendous stress. How could I allow the other person off the hook for causing me so much pain? I wanted justice.

I was in a victim mentality without even realizing it. I didn't know any better. The world around me survived in a victim mentality. Being the victim was how attention was dished out on a silver platter. But in reality, that platter was not a silver platter, but glass that could crack and shatter at any moment.

Above All, be the heroine of your life, not the victim.

–Nora Ephron

I'd also grown up believing that to forgive projected a sense of weakness. When someone hurt you, you were never to forgive them. Maybe you would say all was forgiven, but inside you knew better. If you forgave, you would allow the person to betray you again, so you held onto the unforgiveness like a cloak of honor. In reality, there is no honor in it. You are only hurting yourself.

Forgiveness can be very challenging, especially when the transgression is heinous, and yet it is vital. Why? I'll leave it to this famous saying to explain: *"Resentment is like drinking poison and waiting for the other person to die."* And, damn, I drank poison for many years! What about you? How much poison have you had to drink? Are you still drinking it now?

Holding onto anger, resentment, bitterness, and hate take a tremendous toll on us – it drains us physically, emotionally, and mentally. It steals our joy and our ability to move on. It keeps us stuck in and closed off from experiencing the abundance that is our birthright.

Our bodies don't know the difference between the actual and remembered experience, so when we ruminate on pain and betrayal, we are physiologically activating it over and over (essentially, we are going into survival – fight, flight or freeze mode). Moreover, because we get what we focus on, we bring into our reality more situations that absolutely confirm for us that forgiveness isn't right for us, thus perpetuating the vicious cycle of rage and anxiety. The last thing we want is to bring in more painful experiences, or drink the poison and wait for the other person to die.

Note that I am not invalidating the tough emotions we feel when we are wronged. In fact, it's important to experience and process them so we can appreciate positive emotions.

However, it's also important to realize that forgiving some-one does NOT mean you are:

1. condoning their behavior

2. going to be their friend, or

3. have to keep them in your life

Forgiving and letting go is for *your* benefit, not theirs. In fact, they might not even know you've forgiven them. You are simply freeing yourself from the bondage of anger and resent-ment.

Remember: we are not victims, we have choices. Also remember that people in pain hurt others. Their behavior is usually not about you, but a reflection of how they feel about themselves. They too are trying to free themselves from pain, they are just going about it in a highly dys-functional, ineffective, and fucked up way.

That realization has really helped me to forgive. When I con-sider the source, the feelings of anger and bitterness soften. I see that the person must be experiencing tremendous pain, insecurity, shame, fear, and lack within themselves to be able to inflict that type of pain. I begin to feel compassion. Frankly, I have also learned that my own fears may have played a part in the betrayal.

I will give you an example. I had forty thousand dollars stolen from me in a business situation. I was furious! As I reflected on the situation, I realized that I had made the business decision from a vulnerable place. I had just been hurt by someone I loved and was searching for acceptance outside of myself. So when the business opportunity came wrapped up in a pretty package of community, freedom, and abundance, I jumped on it, completely dismissing all the red flags. After a few weeks, however, my intuition began to tug at me. I was feeling that something was off with the business transaction, but because I had already made the commitment and didn't want to seem like a "flake," I went against my better judgment and continued to move forward.

A few months later, after I had gotten much more grounded and gained clarity, I knew with certainty that I had made a mistake and decided to back out of the commitment. When I reached out to the person to let them know, they insisted on meeting me in person to discuss it. I agreed, and again went against my intuition and stayed in the transaction based on the false information they provided. It wasn't until a year later that I discovered the betrayal. I was so furious with them, but even more so with myself. How could this happen to me?! And what kind of person rips off another like that?! The answer: people who are in a place of fear and lack. My higher awareness, my spirit, knew that money is energy and it would come back to me tri-fold; my spirit also knew that the two individuals I was dealing with had experienced tremendous trauma. Now, that doesn't excuse their actions, but it did help me realize that it wasn't about me, but their own fears. And, again, I was in a low place in my life and an energy match to their fear and insecurity ... therefore, a perfect target. So in this case, one of the people I needed to forgive was me. I also learned to never make a major decision when I am in a vulnerable and ungrounded emotional state.

I am in no way saying that it is our fault when we are betrayed or hurt by another. I just want to bring awareness to the fact that we sometimes choose to ignore red flags and that makes us more susceptible to these experiences.

Face it, we all fuck up.

We:

- Stay in relationships longer than we should
- Allow others to take our power or take advantage of us
- Don't speak up when we know we should
- Constantly feel we aren't where we're supposed to be in life
- Believe we are "breaking" so called social or cultural expectations

And when we do any of these things, we judge ourselves harshly, holding ourselves hostage to feelings of guilt. We're so mad at ourselves that we'll do anything we can and use things like hiding behind work, shopping, drinking, drugs, overeating, and other addictions as distractions.

When we do fall into the trap of beating ourselves up over and over for the same mistake, we are sentencing ourselves to a life of unnecessary pain, fear, and judgment, leading to an immense amount of stress and fatigue … and it will hinder our personal growth.

Beating yourself up over your mistakes will never help move you into the energy of joy and peace. Realize that no matter how bad your mistakes are, they allow you to grow. The power lies in reflecting on where you went wrong and committing to doing it differently next time.

The next time you find yourself going a few rounds with your inner self, step back and bring your awareness to your mean self-chatter. Listen to it like you would listen to a child who just made a mistake. Then tell your mean self that you accept the mistake and you're ready to move forward and make better choices.

> *Forgiveness is a gift you give yourself.*
>
> **–Tony Robbins**

This awareness, and your willingness to move forward, will enable you to get closer to forgiving yourself. When you are able to forgive and have compassion for yourself, it becomes much easier to have compassion and forgiveness for others.

If you are unsure how to forgive or move forward, you are not alone. The good news is, you don't need to know the how right now. When you make a commitment and set the intention to forgive, the how will fall into place and the universe will begin to move you toward healing for yourself and your greater good.

Here is one of my favorite quotes from Ajahn Chah, one of Thailand's most famous meditation teachers:

> *If you let go a little, you will have a little happiness. If you let go a lot, you will have a lot of happiness. If you let go completely, you will be free.*

Forgiveness is a process that is unique to each person and unique to each hurtful situation, so go at your own pace. There is one situation that has taken me almost two decades to forgive! Just know when you set the intention to forgive, you will begin to uncover multiple layers of healing. It reminds me of an onion. I am going to envision a red onion because it is sweeter and has a beautiful purple color. You have this beautiful red onion and the forgiveness process starts with the skin ... the intention to forgive and the natural progression of forgiveness begins ... the next layers of healing start and you get a little closer to forgiveness. The anger and rage are still there, but they begin to diminish. Then the next layer of healing begins. And, in all of these different layers of healing there are lessons and levels of awareness tied to the initial grievance we are holding onto.

Now here's something super cool for those of you who are cringing at the thought of forgiving that person that devasted you. You NEVER have to talk to or see them again. You can experience the healing journey of forgiveness without involving them at all. That said, everything is energetic and when you release the hold they have on you don't be surprised if they circle around with an apology or a gesture of remorse. That gesture can also come in a dream or through other sources. Not that we are waiting for that, but just take notice as you begin your forgiveness journey.

I had a friend I loved dearly, but unfortunately there came a point in the relationship where I had to set a boundary. Her reaction to this wasn't very pretty. In fact, it was pretty nasty. I felt tremendous pain from the words she spewed at me. I was upset, hurt, and sad. I felt that I could never trust friendships again. I gave myself time to grieve. In the past I would have had a very hard time forgiving this; however, I realized that her outburst was a reflection of what she was feeling internally. In that moment I had tremendous compassion and was able to forgive her and myself. I had to forgive myself because I had fallen into the same pattern in the past – that of giving too much and not setting my boundaries sooner. I also took accountability for my part in the situation.

We don't have to walk the journey of forgiveness on our own. We always can turn to God or our higher power to support us, especially when we are stuck in our ego and the walls are up around our heart. All we have to do is ask and we will receive the needed support.

There is a tremendous amount of research done on the science of forgiveness. In a white paper written in April of 2020, Dr. Everett L. Worthington, Jr. professor of psychology at Virginia Commonwealth University, outlines a five-step process of forgiveness he calls R.E.A.C.H.

R: Recall the hurt. To forgive and heal, you have to face the pain instead of sweeping it under the rug.

E: Empathy. This is NOT EASY TO HAVE, especially in instances of traumatic experiences and abuse, yet it is so powerful. Put yourself in the other person's shoes. What trauma could they have possibly experienced, and be experiencing within themselves, to inflict such hurt?

A: Altruistic (unselfish) gift. Remember a time when you made a mistake and that person forgave you. We are all human and we all make mistakes. We are making the best decisions in the moment based on the knowledge and resources we have in that moment.

C: Commit. Once you have experienced the journey of forgiveness and you feel free from the hurt, write yourself a note as simple as "I forgive (THEIR NAME) for hurting me." This helps you take your power back and allows the forgiveness to last.

H: Hold onto Forgiveness. Boy, can I relate to his final step! There were many times I went through the forgiveness process and I thought, *Okay, I feel great. I have put this behind me,* only to get triggered and experience those feelings of unforgiveness sprouting up again. This is why Dr. Worthington asks us to write it down – it shows intention and commitment and is therefore more likely to last.

> *Forgiveness is just another name for Freedom.*
> **–Byron Katie**

One forgiveness story I am particularly in awe of is that of Elizabeth Smart. Elizabeth was only fourteen years old when Brian David Mitchell stole her from her home in Salt Lake City, Utah in June of 2002. Elizabeth was held captive in the woods behind her home, where she was sexually abused by her captor and his wife before she was spotted and rescued on the street nine horrible months later. I still cry to this day when Elizabeth, in her TedTalk, quotes something her mother said to her:

> Elizabeth, what these people have done to you is terrible, and there aren't words strong enough to describe how wicked and evil they are. They have stolen nine months of your life away from you that you will never get back but the best punishment you can ever give them is to be happy, is to move forward with your life, to do all the things that you want to do. Because by feeling sorry for yourself, by holding on to

the past, by reliving it, that's only allowing them to steal more of your life away from you and they don't deserve that. They don't deserve a single second more of your life so you need to be happy and move on with your life.

Today Elizabeth Smart is a child safety activist and commentator for ABC News. Her life could have really taken a turn for the worse after that horrific experience, but she made the choice to take her power back and transmute her pain into her greatest potential.

I am just going to keep it real. I know there are going to be things that are very difficult to forgive. Just thinking about forgiving them may make you feel like you are betraying yourself. In those instances, honor your feelings knowing that you absolutely have a right to them. No one can tell you otherwise. Focus on forgiving yourself for the effect the betrayal had on you and navigate the process at your own pace. We are neither Jesus nor Buddha – we are human beings – and it's very important to show ourselves the same compassion we would show others.

Activity

This is such a powerful forgiveness activity I learned from Sunny Dawn Johnston.

Think about someone that you hold negative emotions toward because they hurt you. Now, write them a letter as if you are talking to them. In that letter write everything that you want to say, even if it is hurtful and nasty as fuck! Leave nothing out. Get everything out of your heart and onto the paper. When you're done, put the letter away for twenty-four hours, then come back to it the next day. Ask yourself if there is anything left that you want to say to the person. If so, write it down. If not, time to burn the letter! I typically burn the letters in my kitchen sink. Once you burn the letter, take a deep breath, blow it out and say, "I choose peace of mind, freedom, and joy." After you burn and release, make sure to do something for yourself that makes you feel good.

Chapter Four

Your Judgement is a Reflection of Your Own Sh*t!

When you judge another you do not define them,
you define yourself.

–Wayne Dyer

I rarely watch the news, but during the Pandemic of 2020, I sat, my heart breaking, as I witnessed the absolute chaos erupting in our country.

Millions had lost their income after shelter-in-place orders had forced thousands of businesses to close. Schools were shuttered as well, which meant parents were now scrambling to oversee their children's education at home. People were depressed, stressed, scared, and feeling vulnerable.

I was feeling the dense energy of the hate, bias, and judgment that was pouring out everywhere I turned; it was profound. How could we be "one nation under God," and yet be so divided and separated? People were being judged for the color of their skin, for their affiliations, for their opinion, for their choices, for what they did and for what they didn't do. Name it, and there was a judgment to be had. The pain and trauma of the collective had exploded, and rightfully so. We were in a crisis of humanity.

What I realized during that time is that hate and bias are rooted in deep judgment. Judgment is separation.

We all make judgments. Like fear, it is a natural instinct and part of our brain's protection mechanism. And, like fear, it has its place, for example, when we make a discernment about a potentially risky situation. However, also like fear, judgment often runs amuck. When we are judging another, it comes from a place of fear and insecurity. We may be fearful of becoming the person we are judging. We are judging our own shadows.

As Karen Casey wrote in her book, *Let Go Now,* "There are two kinds of business: your business and none of your business." Other people's lives and what they choose to do with them is really none of our business. Yes, we care about the people we love and we want the best for them. We can absolutely make an effort to guide, influence, and set the best example, but we cannot in any way, shape, or form control the decisions of another. And judging them isn't helping us or them, because judgment separates us from love. When we separate from love it creates an ugly feeling within us. Pay attention next time you judge yourself or someone else. How does it feel? I can almost guarantee you that it doesn't feel good. There is a small feeling inside that knows that something is off.

There is a saying in Arabic I use all the time and my friends laugh their assess off and now they have begun to use it. I say Khalee'hun Mabsuteen. Meaning: hey, if you witness someone doing something that brings them joy, even if it makes no sense to us and we judge it … khalee'hun Mabsuteen meaning …

leave them alone in their happiness and joy. Don't rain on their parade!

Can we have an opinion? Of course. Can we have a preference? Absolutely. The difference is that we are honoring what we prefer (i.e., agreeing to disagree) without dishonoring (judging) another's. Remember, our beliefs are based on imprints and experiences from childhood, and ninety-five percent of the way we live our lives is based on those unconscious beliefs. Thank goodness we can gain awareness and begin dismantling those unconscious beliefs by creating more empowering, loving beliefs. Some people may choose to stay stuck in their current belief system and that is something we also have to accept. Judging them for where they are in their journey doesn't make us any better. They are here to teach us too!

Growing up, I saw a lot of judgment being handed out. It wasn't good or bad, it just was. *Why did he/she buy this car, that's stupid. Why did she wear that dress? It's ugly. Why did he go to that restaurant? That restaurant sucks.* There is truth to the saying, "Different strokes for different folks," my friend! We are all created with unique tastes, likes, desires, and wants. Can you imagine how boring the world would be if we were all the same? Just because I like the Chinese restaurant down the street and you like the one across the street doesn't make me an idiot. It's just my preference. Silly example, I know, but I think you get my gist.

I have learned that when I find myself having a judgmental thought to immediately get curious. I witness my judgment instead of engaging in it. I know my judgment really isn't about the other person. It is about my own beliefs, fears, insecurities, opinions, and preferences.

I ask myself what about the person or situation is triggering me. Our life experiences shape our belief system and we unconsciously hold the notion that our beliefs are the right ones. This is a funny little story. I have a friend who has argued with me on many occasions that women over forty SHOULD NOT wear two-piece bathing suits. WHAT? By age forty we have typically worked really hard to own ourselves and step into our worth and if we want to wear a two-piece, I say, "Work it! That is fabulous!" Yet to my friend, that is a legit belief. Now I can judge her for it and she can judge me, but instead we laugh and realize neither of us is right or wrong – it's just our opinion. Someone else told me that a woman over the age of fifty who has long hair is trying to be young and should get over it. I laugh at the one, too, because I will likely have long hair until you put me in the grave at a hundred.

Judgment and criticism come from a place of fear.
Choose Courage instead.

–Unknown

You see, we judge others based on our own belief systems, which, again, were imprinted on us before we were able to make our own informed decisions. We feel uncomfortable and upset when others judge us, yet we do the same. When we are in a place where we are feeling insecure and unworthy it makes us feel better to judge others and their shit, but really that's an illusion, a false sense of security.

Remember, our ego's job is to protect us and keep us safe. I have learned to work with my ego, honor its fears, and remind it that we are okay – that we don't need to judge in order to feel better about ourselves. When we are in judgment we are in a place of resistance. When we are in a place of resistance, we are not allowing the flow of life's magical possibilities to come our way. Judgment closes off our ability to attract what we want because we are focusing on all the aspects of life that we don't want. Judgment blocks our ability to receive. When we are in judgment, we are draining our energy and separating from love.

I used to get really down on myself when my mind would go to judgment. I felt like a bad person. Now my mind doesn't stay on judgment but for a split second. I have learned to appreciate my judgment because the judgment isn't about the other person at all; it is about me. I get curious and ask myself, "What unhealed part of me is the person triggering?" I have also learned not to judge myself for having judgmental thoughts, but to witness them without engaging. I have come to see judgment, not as a bad thing, but an opportunity to learn, heal, and grow.

As I have done my own inner work, stepped into my higher self, owned who I am, learned my worth and to love myself unconditionally, judgment has turned into acceptance. When we love and accept ourselves, the more freely we love and accept other people and situations for what they are. We see the beauty in our differences, understanding that we are all on our own unique, imperfect journey. We make mistakes. We hurt others. We hurt ourselves. We hurt the people we love, all because we are hurt and afraid. We judge ourselves much harder than we judge anyone else.

Again, this is our inner critic, or mean girl, judging us for what we should do, what we could do, and what we don't have. We compare ourselves to everyone who has what we want and beat ourselves up for not being where we want to be. Do you ever take a minute to just be satisfied where you are? Or are you always ruminating on how you could have done more or better? When we hold that type of judgment towards ourselves, we project it out to the world. Typically, our inner mean girl is never satisfied and constantly judging, but we can teach her how to work with us. We can acknowledge her and guide her. She is trying to do her best for us and when we honor her and thank her, her judgy, bitchy voice doesn't ring as loud. She really just wants to be heard because her job is to protect us from looking like an idiot. What she doesn't realize is that we are smart and we have wisdom, tools, and resources that can support us in gentler, more positive ways and that she is more than welcome to come along in a new and empowering way as well.

I have been judged from the time I can remember. I still get judged and will always get judged. For example, I'm often judged for putting my vulnerability on social media. They believe it is weak, that we should keep our emotions close to the vest. When I hear these things, I just remind myself, *Grace don't take it personally. This isn't about you. It's about his or her own beliefs and you're challenging that belief.* I also respect their perspective because that is their perspective and who am I to judge someone else's reality?

One of the hardest things I have had to accept is that not everyone is at the same place in their journey as I am. I want to shake them and say, "Hey, that belief is holding you back. The story you are telling yourself based on that belief isn't true! You are not weak to show your vulnerability, in fact, it is brave and courageous. And if you do, you will feel so much better and live in so much joy. But that's not my place. As I said before, we can guide and influence, but we cannot control.

When you are face-to-face with a judgmental, critical, person please don't take it personally. Fact: we only take it personally because we already have a fear that what they are saying is true. OUCH! This is why cultivating unconditional self-worth is critical to our well-being. Remind yourself that if the person is talking to you in such a critical way because that is how they talk to themselves. No, that doesn't make it okay, and you don't have to accept it. You can set your boundaries, just know it's not about you.

(Note: Your external experiences are a mirror of your inner world; therefore, if you are judgy and salty you're going to attract a plethora of judgy and salty people into your life. Be aware of how you show up! Be honest with yourself.)

We can absolutely be open to constructive feedback, but be very discerning about who you accept that criticism from. Then be aware of that person's own beliefs, because typically people are offering feedback from their own frame of reference. You can always say, "Thank you, I appreciate the feedback," but you don't have to internalize it.

Judgment – my own and others' – ruled my life for many years. That was an exhausting, miserable way to live, and I can honestly say I spent more time in anxiety than in joy. Nothing was EVER good enough. My godsister Mimi and I used to complain to our mothers that their book of what will shame the family was as long and daunting as a set of encyclopedias. To say I am grateful to have shifted away from that limiting mindset is an understatement! Freedom from others' judgment and living your life on your terms feels euphoric.

*The greatest prison we live in is the prison of
what other people think.*

–Sunny Dawn Johnston

The best place to start healing from self-judgment is to forgive yourself for judging yourself. Many of us suffer from some form of perfectionism. It most likely stems from a mistake we made as children, the consequence of which was painful and humiliating. Oh, I sure can remember many! As a young adult I hated making mistakes because I felt it meant I was a complete and utter failure. While in my advanced coaching certification classes, I learned that there is no failure – only feedback. That was such an aha moment for me. How I wish I had known this earlier in life – I would have saved myself so much heartache. Our "failures" are our greatest teaching moments. My goodness, when a toddler is learning how to walk would you beat her up and judge her when she stands up and falls on her booty? Of course not! She is learning and is going to fall many times before she starts walking with confidence.

We hold onto the unrealistic and damaging notion that we are only worthy if we are perfect and proceed to judge ourselves for all our imperfections. If you want to live a miserable life, continue striving for that perfection. I am here to tell you it doesn't exist. Why? Because as human beings we are constantly growing and expanding. We are alive and our spirit soars when we are in a constant state of growth and improvement.

I do have high standards and want to achieve excellence, or at least be the best that I can. Self-sabotage uncovers itself and starts doing the happy dance when you base your worth on what you are accomplishing. Here we are back at judgment once again. It wasn't good enough. *OMG, look at what she has done. I am a loser because I should be as far along as her.* Just STOP!

You know what your intention and agenda are. You know if you are putting sincere action and effort into your life. You know if you are doing the bare minimum to get by. Take some time to get curious, get real and raw with yourself, and examine your self-judgment. Yes, girl, that can be very painful, but it is also where the magic happens. When we bravely choose to sit in our pain and feel it, own it, and commit to change, the pain starts to shift and release us from its claws. When you love yourself for who you are, when you know you are un-conditionally worthy, and when you accept yourself for your imperfections and flaws, you begin to connect to your true authentic self. You aren't scared when the mask starts to come off and the veil is lifted. You are in the flow. You see yourself – as well as others – through the loving eyes of our all-knowing Creator. There is no separation.

We are all part of the same race – the *human race.* We're all created in the image of our mighty Creator. We also all have a need to be seen, heard, respected, and loved. I am no different from you, and you are no different from me.

We want to be part of the greater change; however, we don't know where to start or what to do. We CAN be the small pebble in the pond that creates a greater ripple. Below are a few concepts that you can practice to help create a more loving and kinder world. It really does start with us.

1. Turn inward

We all have biases. As uncomfortable as it is, be introspective and start to recognize your own bias and judgment. Being aware of your bias is the first step to educating yourself, so get curious.

2. Start within your own home and circles

If you're in a situation where inappropriate or judgmental comments are made, step up and speak up. Yes, it's uncomfortable and messy, but growth doesn't come from a comfortable place. We can have these conversations in a respectful way; it doesn't have to be hurtful or hateful. Be that leader and influencer in your circle.

3. Commit to love

Make an effort to show up in a loving, kind, and compassionate way. We are human and there will be times when we fall into anger and judgment. But you can always choose again. Get back to love.

4. Practice Empathy

Empathy is realizing that each person we encounter is responding from their own fears, pains, and insecurities. Hurt people hurt people. This is not an excuse, just a reminder to consider the source.

Activity

Today, get curious and get real about your own judgment. Write down five judgments that you hold and for each one ask yourself, "Is that true?" Your unconscious mind will start bringing examples to you to debunk your judgment. True story!

Chapter Five

You Are SO P.H.A.T.
(Pretty, Hot, And Tempting!)

*You define beauty yourself. Society doesn't
define your beauty.*

–Lady Gaga

You are ugly! You are fat! Your skin is too white! You are too short! Your nose and forehead are too big! Your hair is too curly/frizzy. Your butt looks like a cow from Holland!

These are the messages I heard as a young girl about my body. These are the messages I internalized and began repeating in my mind over and over until I believed them as the absolute TRUTH. Yet each and every day of my life my body has been loyal to me because it wakes me up every morning to a new day. My body has carried me through the most challenging of days. It kept me moving forward when I wanted to lie down and tap the fuck out. I have pushed my body and let it go without, yet it continues to show up even when it felt depleted and SHE wanted to throw in the towel. Even when I abused her with toxins like bad food, alcohol, drugs, and cigarettes she still pulled through even though she was screaming, "Don't put that crap in me!"

My dearest, sweetest, loving, badass, loyal, down-as-fuck body, I am so sorry! Please forgive me for all the abuse and pain I have imposed on you!

Would I ever treat anyone the way I treated my body? Absofuckinglutely NOT, and I'm sure you wouldn't treat anyone that way either! Yet our bodies faithfully continue to wake us up each day and carry us through a full schedule. As resilient and miraculous as our bodies are, however, they will begin to crash and cry for help if we continue to abuse and berate them.

Taking care of ourselves emotionally, mentally, and physically is critical to our overall health. Our mind, spirit, and body are all connected. There is no separation. What our mind and spirit think is felt through our body. Our body is one of the vessels that speaks to us when we are off track. Those headaches, neckaches, stomach aches, and other aches are signals from our bodies that we need to look closer to making changes. All of our emotions and life experiences are held in our bodies. When we are out of alignment, ungrounded, and have unprocessed emotions our body absorbs it all, eventually leading to illness and disease. It is absolutely critical to move the dense energy out of your body to move toward creating optimal health. How would it feel to you if you had to carry a heavy bag of rocks on your back 24/7, three hundred sixty-five days a year? Well, that's what we do to our bodies when we internalize our emotions instead of releasing them.

Embrace and love your body. It is the most amazing thing you will ever own.

–Unknown

One way that we can help move and clear the unresolved emotions from our body is through movement – it as important as food and water. Exercise is one of the best anti-depressants. When you get your body moving for just ten minutes, you are activating endorphins and changing your emotional state. I can hear you moaning about how you don't have time to exercise. My dear, sweet friend, you CAN'T NOT make the time to get moving. I will tell you why. Because consistent exercise shifts your emotional state, helps release emotional resistance, and increases your energy – and when your energy is increased and your endorphins have kicked in, you will be more productive and focused!

A universal goal among my hundreds of coaching clients is to be more productive and focused. Don't have a gym membership, you say? Not a problem, you don't need one to get your body moving. There are plenty of ways to do this: walking, dancing, jogging outside or in place, climbing stairs, doing jumping jacks… the list goes on and on.

Nature is one of the most amazing gyms there is, as well as an incredible force for healing. Pre-pandemic, I would rarely if ever go outside. During the pandemic the gyms were closed so I was forced to get outside. I never realized how healing being in nature can be. Now I get outside several times a week, especially when I find myself feeling out of balance. Even a thirty-minute walk by the water changes the way I feel in my body and about my body. Plus, I get my daily requirement of vitamin D.

One study from the University of Exeter Medical School in England sited: "A lack of exposure to natural surroundings may be one of the causes behind many modern ills."

Staying stagnant has a major impact on our physical *and* mental health. Studies have shown that committing to an exercise lifestyle can not only boost your immune system, it reduces the risk of developing type 2 diabetes and high blood pressure.

As I mentioned earlier, it's also a fabulous antidote for depression and anxiety. When we move our bodies, we release feel-good endorphins. They boost our energy levels, blood circulation, and overall confidence. We get a healthy glow that comes from the inside out – one you definitely can't get with Botox!

As mentioned, after my mother's death a lot more responsibility fell on my shoulders. That, coupled with the fact that I had my youngest son one month later, resulted in severe postpartum depression. I was always exhausted, very sad, and cried a lot from the grief and stress. My body felt so heavy, like I was carrying a ton of bricks. Some days it was VERY difficult to get up but I had to. I pushed my body through the horrible emotional pain I was experiencing. When I went to elder family members to let them know I needed support because something wasn't right with me, they would say, "Don't worry, just be strong and suck it up. You are fine." But I wasn't fine, and I decided to seek medical support. When he suggested an antidepressant, I believed I had no other choice and I started the medication. They helped for two years... until I found myself crying uncontrollably that day in the doctor's office. Intuitively I knew that the medication was no longer working for me and it was time to explore other options. Exercise was one of them, and it helped pull me out of a very dark and scary place. Now, I am not a doctor and I don't recommend stopping your medications if that is what is currently supporting you. I am just sharing my experience.

Fact: no matter how healthy we are, we all go through really stressful times. Moving our bodies keeps us grounded and connected to the creative side of our brains. This helps us identify solutions, rather than being stuck in a lethargic, "frozen" state.

I understand thinking about starting an exercise program can be scary. The time commitment. The financial commitment. Driving to the gym or studio. Feeling self-conscious about even being in the gym. When we think about all these factors at once, it can be overwhelming. But it doesn't have to be. You don't have to start with an hour or thirty-minute workout; start with just fifteen minutes a day. Go for a walk or bike ride around your neighborhood, or put on your favorite playlist at home and dance it out. You could also jump on YouTube and find a workout routine that matches your skill level and interests – there are thousands to choose from.

The key to reaping the benefits of exercise is to make it a daily habit. This requires commitment and discipline. I recommend you calendar it into your schedule; otherwise, it may not get done. Again, start with fifteen minutes a day for two weeks, then increase it to thirty to sixty minutes a day for two weeks. And yes, it is okay if you skip a day here and there. It won't kill you.

Okay, I hear all the excuses you are making in your head – and here's the deal: it's all on you. Ask yourself, if exercising is going to provide you with amazing benefits like increased energy and reduced anxiety – the very things you desire – why wouldn't you commit to incorporating it into your life? Sit quietly with yourself and really dig deep and ask yourself the question. What's stopping you from committing to thirty to sixty minutes of exercise three days a week to improve the quality of your life and to show your body that you love and appreciate her?

Recently one of my close friends joined a local studio. She realized the only way she was going to commit to a workout is if she paid for it upfront each month. She called me a week in and told me that she finally understood why I was so committed to moving my body every morning. She was feeling great. There were a few mornings that she went to the class feeling frustrated and stressed. After her thirty-minute workout she felt much lighter emotionally and she was excited to start her day. Just this morning, my son came into my room after going to the gym. He said, "When I went to the gym this morning, I was so tired I didn't feel like being there... and now I feel so good!" When we practice healthy habits, we are being an example to our loved ones and that begins to create an impact!

I hated gym class during elementary school and high school. I was very insecure and felt uncoordinated, fat, and stupid. I was the last person to be picked for any sports activity and that made me feel like a loser. So of course, as a young girl I had resistance around moving my body. It wasn't until I was nineteen that something clicked and I started to exercise off and on. I was a new mom battling postpartum depression, a very stressful career, and toxic personal life, and I now KNOW that exercise really saved my life and my body. When my first son was born, I made a conscious commitment to exercising. Gaining fifty pounds was a motivator, because in the world I lived in size zeroes and twos were celebrated, not size fourteens.

Being on a diet since the age of ten, I was obsessed with the scale and felt very depressed and self-conscious about my body more than ever after I gave birth to my first son ... especially since when I got married the rumor was that my husband would leave me when I got old, fat, and ugly. Yes, people are fucked up, and their words haunted me for years.

I had gym memberships for ten years prior but wasn't really consistent. I'd rather go eat and drink after work than get a workout in. Having a business to run, a newborn baby, a husband, and tons of family drama, I thought to myself how the FUCK am I going to find time to exercise? I felt like I barely had time to breathe. When you want something bad enough you make it work. I ordered Cher and Tae Bo workout videos (yes, totally dating myself) and no matter how exhausted I was at the end of the day I would pop them into the VCR and just move. Some days I would just put my son in the playpen and he would watch me looking silly as FUCK as I jumped around the living room.

I stayed committed and consistent to the daily workouts and eventually I started looking forward to the workouts. Then I went back to a gym that was open twenty-four hours, going after putting my son down at night. I had a friend that would join me, which was wonderful – a playdate and workout in one.

Within twelve months I had released the fifty pounds I gained during my pregnancy. I had more energy than I had before and I was feeling much better emotionally. Little did I know was I needed that energy and grounded emotional state to walk my mother through her journey with cancer and through her transition out of this lifetime. See, the Universe works in mysterious ways, always preparing you for what lies ahead.

Notes: in the stories I just shared I wasn't motivated to exercise because I loved my body and wanted to keep it healthy. My motivation was that I didn't like my body and believed it needed to be a size two to be good enough.

Learn to embrace your own unique beauty, celebrate your unique gifts with confidence. Your imperfections are actually a gift.

–Kerry Washington

I will never be a size two. God didn't create my body that way. I am a five-foot-two, voluptuous woman with a size ten foot. I need my big feet to carry my hips which are too big for my short frame. Today I embrace my body in all its glory. It wasn't an easy process, and it took years for me to get where I am today. And I'd be fronting if told there isn't the critical voice in my head that comes up and talks shit to me. She's still there, questioning the cellulite and fat on my thighs – "Can't you work harder to get rid of that?" It questions the fat under my arms, on my hips, and booty. I tell the mean girl, "Hey, I hear you, sister, but we are beautiful just the way we are!"

Over a period of twenty-plus years I tried every diet there was. I think there was something called the cabbage diet where you just ate cabbage soup for days. The Suzanne Somers diet ... I bought all her books. The South Beach diet. The Dolly Parton, eat one bite of whatever you want diet ... the list is endless. Today I can't look at a rice cracker without feeling stressed! I dreaded going out to dinner or to celebrations because there would be food there that wasn't on my list. One time I went to the cabin with the girls during the winter and we were stuck there all weekend. These girls were eating some bomb food like chips, Oreos, nuts, Wonder bread, and cheese sandwiches ...

and there I was with my fifty-pound bag of baby carrots. Talk about torture. Today I laugh out loud at that memory. My focus on food and what to eat and what not to eat overshadowed the fun I could have been having on MANY occasions. Instead of being present in the moment I was ruminating on what I could eat, how many calories I already ate, and how miserable it felt not to eat the delicious food in front of me, missing opportunities to laugh, feel joy, and connect in the process. I wasn't only torturing my mind, I was torturing my soul and torturing my body.

It tortures our soul because our soul loves the ecstasy that delicious foods create when we eat them! Can you tell I love food? When we eat foods we enjoy, it nourishes our soul. When we deprive ourselves of the foods we enjoy, our soul cries for some tender-loving deliciousness.

It tortures our body because our body was created to be fueled with nutritious real foods. Not fake foods like rice crackers, non-fat cream cheese, and protein bars. Being constantly focused on what you put in your mouth and how many calories you are eating clogs your mind and puts you in a place of resistance. Your mind understands your focus on food and calories as lack and, as a result, your body holds on to every calorie you're eating for dear life.

I am not going to talk to you about what to eat and what not to eat. This chapter isn't about a diet or losing weight. The point I would like to get across is that our mind, soul, and body are connected and when we abuse our bodies, we are abusing our mind and soul.

Healing my relationships with food and my body has been a long journey that I continue to walk each day. Through each layer of healing, I have created new, healthier habits as the years progress. I have realized that I used food to comfort myself during my depressive episodes. Today I still use food to comfort me during my fucked-up days; however, I do it very consciously. I honor myself and give myself permission to enjoy pizza, chocolate, fries, and whatever else I want. Instead of feeling guilty I remind myself that I am nourishing my soul. Eating from a place of love and consciousness is very different than eating from a place of anger, fear, and judgment. I learned this concept from *The Joshua Diet* by Gary Bodley. The book has absolutely nothing to do with diets and everything to do with our energy, mindset, and self-talk around food and our body.

It is a known fact that our weight can be tied to our emotional traumas. As we begin to heal our trauma it is very likely that we begin to release our extra weight. Remember I mentioned that our body absorbs and holds onto all of our emotions. I had been working with one client for a few years. She consistently battled with her weight since childhood. She was such a brave woman. Each week she would show up ready to dig deep into her unconscious beliefs and painful experiences that shaped the way she lived her life. What she noticed was as she started to become aware of her unconscious limiting beliefs, reframe them into more powerful beliefs, and face her painful memories and release them she noticed that she started to release weight.

Not only was she releasing weight she was looking healthier. She showed me a picture of herself from two years prior and a present picture and she looked years younger now than before.

When we begin to heal, become aware, and shift our stories we become lighter. We allow ourselves more space and freedom and that space and freedom helps our internal light to shine brighter. I truly believe healing and living as healthy as we can is the fountain of youth.

Our beauty doesn't come from the size or shape of our bodies. Our beauty radiates from the inside out. When we are fearless and begin to dive into our shit and release what doesn't serve us to create more empowering stories, we transform ourselves from the inside out. Our body responds to our emotional, mental, and spiritual state. When we are more loving and kind to ourselves we are going to naturally be more loving and kind to our bodies. That's when our mind, body, and spirit connection work together for us to live our lives to the fullest. Our body is our temple and the more emotionally & spiritually healthy we get our body will follow and we will make better choices on how we treat our body. Eating healthier food and moving our body will be something we want to do not a difficult choice we feel we have to make. Don't get me wrong I love eating delicious food but now that I am in tune with my body and aware my body tells me what it wants and what it doesn't want. My cravings aren't as strong and I gain my emotional support from community, meditation, and faith instead of from food.

You have been criticizing yourself for years and it hasn't worked. Try approving of yourself and see what happens.

–Louise Hay

One challenging but highly effective tool that helped me reframe my thoughts around my body was mirror work. I would stand in front of the mirror and start thanking every part of my body for the role it played in my life. My eyes to see. My arms to lift my children. My legs to get me from here to here. My hips that carried my children, and so on. This helped me take the focus off the parts of my body that I struggled with. When I started to give consistent love to those parts of my body something strange happened. I wasn't focused on the cellulite on the back of my ass or thigh or focused on how big my butt and hips were. My perception of my body changed. I was just so grateful to wake up every day with a body that functioned and felt great. Today when I do fall back into my old patterns of body shaming or body dysmorphia, I realize that there is a slight change that needs to be made in my mindset and lifestyle and I commit to getting back in alignment. It's about progress, not perfection.

Make today the day that you start a love affair with your own body. Love it, cherish it, take care of it, embrace it, and honor it. Your soul chose this body in which to have the human experience. Our bodies are a miracle. All of our internal systems work together to keep us alive each and every day and we don't even have to think about it. I know it isn't an easy process to accept our bodies, especially since so many commercials and ads target our vulnerabilities; however, committing to one small step can help get you on your way to embracing and loving the most important thing you own forever: YOUR BODY!

I encourage you to make that small step (the activity below) because, girl, you are **P.H.A.T.** (Pretty, Hot And Tempting) and it's time to OWN it!

Activity

Stand in the mirror each morning for the next twenty days and talk to your body the way you would a small innocent child. Give your body love. Tell it how much you love it. How you appreciate it. How you appreciate it always carrying you. Pour words of love and affirmation on your legs, arms, breasts, hips, booty! Your body is your temple. It gets you up every day regardless of how you treat it! Love on it sister because it is your precious temple!

Chapter Six

The Stories You Tell Yourself Are BullSh*t!

Belief becomes the source of your limitation or your liberation. It doesn't matter what's true, it matters what you believe.

–Marie Forleo

For years I was busting my ass and living my life the best way I knew how. I was focused, disciplined, and committed to most of the principles in the hundreds of self-development books I had been reading since the age of fifteen. I thought I had it down pretty good. I hustled and worked my ass off, made an effort to be everything to everyone, and was in constant over-achiever mode. That was what I learned: hustle hard, put the time in, and be marketable (be everything to everyone). I ended up marrying a kind man who valued me, we had kids who were healthy and sound, and I was running a successful business. I was at a point in my life where I had achieved the goals I had set in my early twenties! Amazing, right? WRONG!

I was completely depleted and exhausted. Though I had everything I had dreamed of, in the deepest, darkest part of me something felt very off. I was still struggling within the confines of the prison in my mind. Little did I know I was unconsciously "killing" myself because of the beliefs I was attached to. I would have never imagined my belief system was keeping me exhausted and depleted. WHAT THE FUCK! I was doing all the right things I was told to do to achieve a great life.

During all my years of being submerged in the world of self-development, years of therapy and investing in my own business coaches, the term "limiting belief" had never come up. To this day I am fucking baffled about that, though I have come to accept the fact that I wasn't ready to learn about limiting beliefs, just like I wasn't ready to learn about gratitude. In fact, I am almost certain I *did* read about limiting beliefs; however, my unconscious mind chose not to retain that part of the subject matter. Tony Robbins was one of my favorite motivational speakers, and he constantly talks about the belief system, yet I still never "heard" it. Bottom line: my ego wasn't ready to face my belief system, which was fucked up but served me at the time.

Now, to be fair to myself, our society has conditioned us to believe that overachieving and working long hours is the way to become successful. The books I was reading were emphasizing hustle and grind as a badge of honor. Of course we need to take action to create; however, it doesn't need to be a constant hustle and grind. I believe that this false narrative is cross-cultural. Through having hundreds of conversations with clients, colleagues, and friends, I've learned that many of us are human doings and attaching our worth to how much we do and achieve. Again, not our fault – we have been conditioned that way. Know this: we can change the status quo and create from a place of faith and confidence instead of a place of lack and fear.

Our belief system is what creates our reality. As long as I held on to that hustle-and-grind belief system, I would always be exhausted, depleted, have the perception that I am a step behind, and feeling not good enough. My belief system would keep me on the hamster wheel busting my ass to continue to be successful (Although I really didn't view myself as successful). My belief system would keep me trying to be everything to everyone just to be worthy and a good person. I was in classic self-sabotaging behavior. I had been in 20-plus years of therapy; I had a bachelor's and master's degree and was very successful, yet I had no idea I was in a cycle of self-sabotage. I thought I was doing all the right things to achieve the American vision of success. Boy, was I WRONG! In my mind, I legitimately believed I was doing and giving one hundred percent to live my best life.

As I reflect back, I realize that I needed to go through the experiences I did to grow and expand spiritually. I'm not of the mindset that we need to struggle and experience trauma to grow and expand; however, I do believe that to grow we need to experience some adversity and dive into our shadows to explore the contrast between joy and pain. Without the contrast of pain, we wouldn't know how intoxicating joy feels. Each person's struggle is unique to them and the struggle doesn't have to be extremely traumatic to create an impact in our lives.

I always like to come back to the metaphor of the caterpillar. The caterpillar crawls into the darkness to undertake a paramount transformation to emerge a majestic elegant beautiful butterfly. Those years, I was entrenched in my belief system I liken to the caterpillar in the cocoon … I was going through the steps toward a paramount transformation. When we are in our struggle, in the darkness and depleted, our soul takes us on a journey to really dig down deep. When we are comfortable, we rarely dig deep. It's when we get so uncomfortable that we can't take it anymore that we begin to question our way of life. The belief system that helped me reach the level of success society said I should reach had worked for me, until one day it just didn't.

We have both limiting beliefs and empowering beliefs. We can create a belief based on something we heard on the TV, we can create a belief from something we heard in school, we can create a belief from something we hear our parents say – the list is endless. A belief can be created from a thought that is thought over and over, and a belief can be created from one impactful moment. A belief is a thought we believe to be absolutely true; however, more often than not the belief is FALSE and thus limiting us from stepping into our magnificence and FREEDOM!

Early in life, limiting beliefs serve us – they are our ego's way of keeping us safe. The belief we create gets us what we want so we can feel good or think we are enough. However, as we get older, those beliefs that once served us begin to hold us back, make us sick, and keep us from achieving our greatest potential. These misconceptions can also create depression, anxiety, and feelings of worthlessness – as well as illness and disease in our bodies.

Remember also that these beliefs activate our childhood trauma. When our body gets activated and in a fight, flight, or freeze response, it is because we are having a trauma response to a need that wasn't met as a child. We get kicked into survival mode and we create beliefs based on our traumatic experiences to help keep us safe. Now, a trauma could be as simple as getting lost in the grocery store as a child to major trauma like being abducted from your home like Elizabeth Smart was. We all carry childhood wounds and those wounds, coupled with our limiting beliefs, cause havoc in our lives. The good news is that as we uncover our skewed stories, we also begin to unearth our painful childhood wounds – and, if we are in a state of consciousness, recognize an opportunity to heal them. We become a witness to our mean girl voice and insecurities instead of continuing to be a victim of them. Disclaimer: Our triggers from our childhood wounds can't be avoided; they will continue to prick us like thorns on a rose until we gain awareness, recognize our patterns, and choose to do that deep healing work.

I was working with a client who felt that she had to do everything for everyone. She felt she was doing it out of the kindness of her heart – and she was. Unconsciously, however, there was another motive behind her excessive giving. As I guided her back to her childhood, one particular memory from when she was seven or eight years old emerged. One of our main needs as humans is to be seen and acknowledged – that is how we know we are loved – but as one of ten children, she didn't feel that way. In revisiting that time, she noticed that when she helped her mother around the house or helped her siblings keep their rooms clean, she was praised and acknowledged. This formed a belief within her that she needed to do for others in order to get her needs met – in other words, overdoing became her trauma response and, in her adult life, had led to exhaustion, resentment, and depletion. As I said earlier, we cannot seek validation outside ourselves, nor can we give from an empty cup. From this new perspective, she was able to shift that limiting belief to a more empowering one.

You have the ability to quickly change your patterns of thought, and eventually your life experience.

–Abraham Hicks

I am going to share another one of my limiting beliefs: that if I played, rested, or had fun, I was being lazy and would end up broke. That lie I told myself went hand-in-hand with the fictional storyline that I had to hustle and grind to be successful and, therefore, worthy. Truth: when we rest, take time for play, and have fun, we are much more productive!

I recently attempted an experiment. I switched my focus from more work to more play. I was having so much damn fun! I traveled, partied, and met amazing new people. I was having more fun in my fifties than I ever did in my youth. During the first five months of the experiment, business wasn't as robust as it was when I was focusing solely on work; however, I stayed true to my experiment. I found examples of successful people who worked less and made more. I knew it could be done, I had no doubt, and I was determined to get into that flow. There were many moments when I felt frustrated, like being in that fun flow of living and being wasn't creating the possibilities I anticipated. I would sit in mediation and ask my higher self, *What's the deal?*

What I realized was I still had resistance around the new, empowering story I created, which was "Working less and playing more creates more." In that moment of awareness, I took a deep breath and allowed myself to feel the fear. I realized that the fear was false. I trusted and believed that if I just let go and trusted the process, the possibilities would manifest. Now I was still working and putting effort and action into my businesses, it simply wasn't my only focus anymore.

I typically set goals, but this time I just wrote out a list of how I wanted to feel: joy, freedom, connection, safe, alive, and full of passion. Whenever I felt that stress in my chest, I allowed myself to breathe into it. I also honored it because for decades that fear had served me, driving me into the hustle of achievement; however, now I was ready for a new way of living. And then – BOOM! – it happened. In the seventh month of my experiment, the floodgates of business opened and the possibilities and opportunities began to flow in. I called one of my mentors, crying tears of joy and nearly unable to breathe (at first she thought something was wrong). I explained what had happened within a matter of forty-eight hours (though it really wasn't just forty-eight hours, but six months of conscious creating): several large deals closed at the same time. In the weeks that followed, the flow continued, AND I continued to focus more on play. That play really was connecting with those I loved and creating fun and memorable experiences. I had diminished my limiting beliefs that you can only be successful through the hustle and grind and that if you stopped for fun, you would lose everything.

Of course, there will be times when we will choose to focus more on business or work and there is nothing wrong with that. I do love work and it inspires me. I just had to take the time to rewire my nervous system to believe with certainty that I could work less, have fun, and still be successful. I also realized in my experiment that I no longer tied my worth to achievement. For the first time in my life, I didn't have a big shiny goal that I was striving for. I realized that my achievements made me feel worthy. Isn't that what society conditions us to believe? Today as I write this, my intention is to continue to enjoy what I am doing while connecting with those I love and creating memories. I absolutely believe that if I am being true to myself and doing what I love the most, which is connecting with people on a deep level, I will absolutely achieve my desires. I also know with certainty that opportunities and possibilities that make me feel fulfilled will appear in divine time. Now there are also times I totally feel inspired to hustle; however, now the hustle feels harmonious instead of like a grind.

It's not always easy to uncover our limiting beliefs because they are very sneaky. It takes time to unravel belief systems, and I truly believe it is an ongoing, even lifelong progress, but one that ultimately leads to the discovery of joy and the truth that we are safe and worthy.

Nothing binds you except your thoughts, nothing limits you except your fear, and nothing controls you except your beliefs.

–Marianne Williamson

I was working with a wonderful, bright, talented young lady. I will call her Rose. Rose hadn't worked in many years and was in a dark place. Now, though, she was at a point in her life where she needed to go back to work. She reached out to me for guidance and she was ready to commit to digging deep and doing the work. We uncovered some of her limiting beliefs around what she believed about work. She believed that no one loved their jobs, and she just couldn't see herself in a job that made her miserable. First, we honored the story she was telling herself for keeping her safe and protected when she needed it. Then we began talking through it and uncovered examples of times she did enjoy her work; we also identified people she knew who enjoyed their work. Eventually, she was able to create a more empowering belief around her own career.

For her next action step, I recommended that she write down what her dream job would look like: the responsibilities she would have, how far the commute would be, what her salary would be, what type of culture the place would have, and anything else she could think of. Then I invited her to feel into her new job like she was already there. What emotions would she feel? Passion, excitement, joy, and connection? What would her days look like? Her homework over the next few weeks was to do the visualization and feel into the emotions as often as possible. Within four weeks Rose had an offer for the job she had been creating in her mind. You may not believe this, but you do have choices.

As I mentioned earlier, our limiting beliefs also are at the core of our judgment of others. Take, for example, the client who always over-gave – she would go into a place of judgment when she noticed others were relaxing and not giving to the extent that she was. Her perception of those people was that they were lazy, they didn't care enough, and they were selfish. Once we brought awareness to this myth, we were able to also recognize that her judgment really wasn't about the other person; if she didn't have the belief about constantly having to do for others, it wouldn't have bothered her to see others taking care of themselves.

I have learned that our limiting beliefs lie hidden in our patterns. Once we become aware of our patterns, we can begin to pull out the shitty stories like weeds. Now, it's not always that easy. Just like weeds they can keep popping up, depending on how tied to our identity they are. Those beliefs take more time, and a lot of practice and consistency, to diminish. I have noticed that each time I am about to level up and expand into a new and exciting part of my life, the core beliefs tied to my identity sprout up again. That's when I stop and remind myself that the belief is false; I thank it for serving its purpose when I needed it, and I step forward with courage and choose the new empowering story I created.

Oftentimes we are attached to the drama that our limiting beliefs create. Believe it or not, drama releases the same feel-good hormones that heroin or opiates can. Wild, right?! That's a reason so many people stay in their pattern behaviors. When I started my major transformation, one of my first goals was to walk away from toxic situations and that wasn't easy because the situations were tied to my identity. I remember this feeling of boredom. I would just be sitting in silence and thinking, *Oh my God, I am going to lose my mind.* What I was actually feeling was peace, which made me uneasy because for decades my nervous system had been conditioned to live in drama. Now I embrace the peace and rarely engage in drama. I have learned to boost my endorphins and dopamine through meaningful connections and conversations. That is my new healthy addiction.

We can often find our limiting beliefs and the patterns associated with them in our relationships. For example, we may leave a relationship in which we are over-giving and not getting back, only to find ourselves in another, similar situation. If you are nodding your head to this, I invite you to take a step back and really get honest with yourself. What are your thoughts surrounding relationships? What are the words you say to yourself? If we don't take the time to get real with ourselves, we will move from one relationship to another and continue to perpetuate our cycle of what isn't working for us. We can use this same example with our careers, health, and so on.

The majority of our beliefs have been handed down from generation to generation, and for past generations it worked because they didn't know any better; however, as we evolve and expand as humans those beliefs no longer serve us.

Whether you think you can or think you can't,
you're right.

–Henry Ford

As we create more empowering beliefs and heal our bullshit stories to create more powerful, healthier stories, we are energetically healing and impacting future generations and the generations that came before us as well.

I want to bring awareness to the fact that you can have the exact same conversation with two different people and those two people will process the conversation in very different ways. They are processing the information based on their own belief system and creating the stories in their mind based on their own unique map of reality. Just as they have a different perception of the story, they will also have a different response based on their triggers—just as you will have different perceptions and responses based on your own triggers.

I absolutely believe that you can still be powerful and limitless, even if you haven't uncovered a plethora of limiting beliefs. When you believe something with absolute conviction and you can feel the desire you have to achieve it, there is nothing that can stop you. Your desire and unwavering commitment to achieving your goal will blow any unconscious limiting belief out of the water. I see people create incredible things without ever uncovering what's holding them back; however, when we do have an awareness to those bullshit stories that play in our mind, we begin to expand in exponential ways, in all areas of our life.

My sweet friend, I want you to know without a doubt that you too can write new powerful stories that will elevate you and help you reach the magnificent potential that lies within you. As a result, you will experience a more joyful, passionate, and fun life that you don't want to run from!

I invite you to think about a situation in your life that is really nagging or troubling you, then write down three beliefs that you hold regarding that situation.

For example:

I really want to be in a relationship and I am not sure why I haven't met the right person yet. It's so frustrating.

Some beliefs you may hold.

There are no good prospects out there.

I will never find the right person.

I am too old and everyone at my age is taken.

Now, if you hold the above beliefs that is what you are going to experience. Go through them and ask yourself, "Is that really, without a doubt, true?" Then think of an example that proves your belief false. At this point I invite you to sit in a five-minute meditation just to allow yourself to process the fact that your belief isn't one hundred percent true. Remember, you have held on to this belief because you felt that it served you. After your five-minute meditation, go back to the three beliefs and create more empowering beliefs. This is what is typically called "reframing our thoughts."

Example

There are wonderful people out there that I haven't met yet.

I am confident that I will meet the right person in divine timing.

I am like fine wine! I just get better with time and there will be someone who appreciates my experience and wisdom!

You got this, Girl! I know it isn't easy to dig deep, but I promise there is freedom on the other side and it can be so fun to create new kick-ass stories! You ARE the author of your life story, so make it a fabulous one!

Chapter Seven

F*CK YES, Money Matters!

Money usually represents so much more than dollars and cents. It is tied with our deepest emotional needs: for love, power, security, independence, control, and self-worth.

–Olivia Mellan

A re you cringing? Does the word money make you flinch and give you that tight feeling in your chest? If so, you are not alone; the word money has such a strange effect on many people. It can make you feel shame and embarrassment if you don't have it and it can make you feel shame and embarrassment if you do have it.

Money can be such a taboo topic. God forbid you ever tell someone how much you make. That's a question you never ask. Yet there are those who feel so comfortable boasting about all the money they have … or, in actuality, don't have.

We begin creating our money stories from the time we are able to understand our ABCs. Like all of our beliefs, those about money are passed down to us from our parents, their parents, and their parents' parents. Yes, that is a tongue twister. It isn't a coincidence that generations of families have lived in poverty and it isn't a coincidence that generations of families have lived in wealth.

I am going to fill you in on a secret, one I wish I had learned a lot sooner than when I was forty-something. Money is energy and we attract it based on our beliefs and based on how we feel about ourselves. WHAT!!! Come on, now! Please stop giving me that mumbo-jumbo, please! Yes, girl, I am serious! That is real talk!

In my twenties, I started focusing on money because that was what I saw all around me. Plus, the prince charming I imagined would come and save me with the mansion and millions hadn't shown up, and at that time the cultural belief was if you weren't married by the time you were twenty you were considered an old maid. (By the time I turned twenty-one I believed my chances of marriage were out the door!) Here is a story that I heard over and over. If you are younger, skinny, have super-model looks, are tall, a good cook, submissive, and not too smart or independent, you will attract a wealthy suitor. From my perspective I was none of those things, so I believed I wasn't good enough and that prince wasn't coming.

In addition, I heard the following conflicting stories: If you didn't have money, you were less than but if you did have money you were a show-off, stuck-up, and greedy! WTF! Yes, as I look back now that was confusing as fuck. It wasn't until many years later that I realized I felt shame when I didn't have money and I felt shame when I did have it.

I was financially successful long before my forties; however, the way that I created my financial success was through beliefs that burned me out and left me feeling unfulfilled. Creating that financial stability came with a price tag. I sacrificed my time and freedom. And I felt that I was taking five steps forward and then ten steps back. The money was coming but it wasn't coming easy and as soon as I was way ahead, something would just come up to set me back … I can see you nodding your head. You know what I am talking about.

I felt that I should be so much further ahead than I was. I felt like I was spinning in circles instead of expanding. Thankfully I had read MANY books on money and success so I knew that if I made enough phone calls and followed the sales metrics, I would create the income I desired. OLD-SCHOOL mentality! Yes, it does require us to take action to create abundance; however, the action doesn't have to be a hardcore grind and hustle 24/7. And that was one of my false narratives I had around money, which left little time for anything else, including fun. Who the hell wants to live like that? Well, I did, and after a good decade I felt exhausted and depleted. Bottom line, my friend: I didn't feel worthy enough to deserve money and abundance. I had to prove my worth and only then I could receive abundance – but I couldn't receive too much because then I would be seen as greedy and a show-off. Such a sad realization but such a profound awareness.

I had been studying the law of attraction for some time and it never dawned on me that money is tied to my self-worth! I understand now that I had to go through and experience all the things I did to be where I am today. To be able to teach from a place of wisdom and life experience. I was great at attracting what I wanted but I had made it very challenging for myself when it didn't have to be.

It was also a struggle for me in my marriage to receive from my husband, especially financially. I had so many lies I told myself around relationships and money that started coming into my awareness as I began the brave and courageous process of digging deep and healing. I had a belief that if I allowed a man to support me financially, he would control me and that terrified me. I witnessed women in controlling, abusive relationships and it was difficult and or impossible for them to leave because the man held the financial handcuffs. Add that story I was telling myself to the belief that I wasn't worthy to receive unless I earned it, and that created an unhealthy and self-sabotaging situation. Sure, it was great to bring in such a great income, but I was creating from a place of fear instead from a place of love and self-worth. That kept me feeling drained and exhausted.

> *When your self-worth goes up.*
> *Your Net worth goes up.*
>
> **–Unknown**

Ladies, there is hope! For so long we have been told to rely on someone else for our financial stability and yes there is nothing wrong with that if that is what you choose. But we are absolutely worthy to both receive from our loved ones and create our own wealth. The moment I owned that I am worthy and receiving abundance is my birthright, the floodgates opened.

Money does matter. Zig Ziglar a famous motivational speaker said, "Money isn't the most important thing in life, but it's reasonably close to oxygen on the 'gotta have it' scale." That quote resonated for me so hard when I first heard it.

As I mentioned earlier, money is energy. Like the ocean never runs out of water and we never run out of oxygen, the Universe never runs out of money. The lack of money is in our minds and tied to our worth and beliefs around receiving.

There are millions of abundant people in the world. Those people aren't smarter than you or have an advantage over you – there is a multitude of stories of those who rose from nothing to create tremendous wealth. They also have the same twenty-four hours in the day that we all have. They understand the law of abundance. We attract abundance based on our thoughts and beliefs. We completely control the amount of abundance we allow into our lives and the amount of abundance we stop dead in its tracks from reaching us. Ask any abundant and financially successful person and they will tell you that they are creating their lives. Ask a person who lives in constant lack and scarcity and they will tell you that they are a victim of random circumstances and have no control over their lives or their ability to attract abundance.

The law of abundance says when we focus on and appreciate what we already have even if it is a mattress on the floor that we sleep on we attract more. When we focus on the lack in our lives, we attract more lack. If we believe that we can't make money we will not make money, if we believe we will always live paycheck to paycheck then we will live paycheck to paycheck. If we believe that money is energy and that abundance flows to us with grace and ease because abundance is our birthright … then you open up the gates to bring money into your life with ease and grace. Sounds crazy I know, but it's law, my friend! Again, we for sure need to take action, but when we realize that abundance is our birthright, opportunities and possibilities begin to show up in our lives.

We must take responsibility for our lives and take responsibility for our money mindset. I am sure you have heard all types of beliefs about money. One that comes up most often is that money is evil. If I believe money is evil then I will stay far away from money as possible and always struggle with money. I will attract negative situations regarding money to prove that money is evil. Money isn't evil, money is energy. People can make bad decisions based on their beliefs around money. It's the people that are creating the undesirable situations, not the money.

I am sure most of you, like myself, want to serve and give back to our community in big ways. Of course, there are hundreds of ways to give back every day. If we are stuck in our lack mentality and trading our valuable time for money, then how much time and energy do we really have to give back the way that our heart desires? I know...I have been there: wanting to spend my time volunteering more than just at my kids' school and wanting to be there for the people I love and spend quality time with them, yet feeling like I had to be handcuffed to my business. I wondered, was it possible to have both time and money?

My dear beautiful friends – the answer is YES! We are created in the image of our powerful Creator. Our spirit didn't come into this body to experience a life of lack. Abundance is our birthright. We came into the world to be abundant and to share our gifts to help humanity grow and expand. We are each other's teachers; however, when we get sucked into the work hard and money doesn't come easy mentality, we begin the cycle of lack and burnout.

Our money situation mirrors our internal dialogue. There are thousands of different limiting beliefs surrounding money. Here are just a few:

"Life is a struggle. It's impossible to get ahead."

"Every time I get ahead something happens and it sets me back again."

"I am not good enough to make that much money."

"If I have a lot of money I won't be accepted or liked."

"Having more money means that I would have to sacrifice my freedom."

"I am not worthy or deserving and who do I think I am to have money."

"Everything is so expensive. How are we every going to survive?"

And the list can go on and on. We created these beliefs totally unconsciously as children or young adults based on the experiences we had and also based on our environment and the beliefs of those we grew up with. Our belief also could have been created from a sixty-second TV commercial. We create these false beliefs around money and live the rest of our lives playing out the false story.

I have heard many financially successful women say that men are intimidated by their financial success and they believe that they will not be able to meet a partner and have a healthy equanimous relationship. This my dear is also a false narrative. There are wonderful men out there that would be so grateful and will appreciate a financially successful woman.

An important key to kicking the shit out of these false narratives is identifying those limiting beliefs and asking yourself, "Is this really true?" Just the slight awareness and questioning the narrative will start a process in your mind to shift it. You have just confused your mind. Wait, what?? Having more money doesn't mean sacrificing your freedom? Having more money actually means you will have more freedom? Now your mind will set out on a search to collect evidence to prove that having more money means more freedom. Before you know it, you will begin witnessing examples of people who have a tremendous amount of money and a tremendous amount of freedom to do what their hearts desire. And evidence that financially successful women do meet wonderful men who value and appreciate their independence.

Surround yourself with people who have unwavering faith in themselves, in You, and in our abundant universe and it will help you take the giant leaps you need to take to get yourself rich.

–Jen Sincero

As women, we have a tremendous amount of shame around money and what I call "Haviness" – my dear friend Tiff T taught me this word and it has stuck with me ever since. Women are givers and we want to comfort and make others feel comfortable. When we are in a position where we may have more than the other person, we begin to feel a sense of shame. We feel guilty for having what we have when the person next to us is struggling to make ends meet. I felt this way for so long. It's so ironic you feel shame for not having enough, then you feel shame for having more than the next person. It feels like we are in a no-win situation. But, again, if you dig deep, it all boils down to our self-worth and self-love. If we know our worth and love ourselves unconditionally, we wouldn't feel the shame in either situation. Having more money or having less money doesn't make us any less than or better than the next person.

We all have the ability to attract abundance. Our attitude and mindset are key. What we focus on we get more of. If we focus on the lack in our lives, we will continue to attract more lack. When we focus on what we have and are grateful for it and appreciate it, we attract more and more of the same.

Each person can also have a different idea of what abundance and having enough is to them. One person may want a mansion on a hill with private staff and there is absolutely nothing wrong with that. If that is their heart's desire, more power to them! Another person may feel abundant with having a cozy studio apartment and all their needs met and have enough time to connect with loved ones and explore new activities. Each person's wants and desires are unique to them and there is no right or wrong. It's what you desire.

I am here to share with you that you can have, do, or be whatever your heart desires when it comes to money and having. The person who is making millions is no more worthy to receive abundance than you are. They just have different beliefs around money and attracting money. You can change your beliefs and rewire your thinking to also attract whatever you desire financially. Your desire point can be five thousand to ninety million dollars, you choose.

You may be wondering, *Do I just believe that money is energy and it will begin to flow in?* Well, yes and no. Will there be times that you will attract money out of the blue? Yes, absolutely. Will there be times that action will need to be taken? Yes, absolutely. There is an exchange of energy with money. It doesn't mean you have to be working in a corporate position or be a small business owner to take action and receive. For the mother who is home caring for the home and children, her actions and her beliefs about money and her self-worth absolutely create an energy exchange for the family. She is receiving through her partner because the energy is one of reciprocity. The child who isn't even old enough to understand the concept of work for money is constantly receiving abundance from parents and loved ones. My point is that receiving abundance is not always a "tit-for-tat" or transactional situation.

Remember, as in nature, there is more than enough abundance to go around. You having it doesn't mean the next person can't also have it. If you have a thriving business and another business similar to yours opens up a mile down the road it doesn't mean that one of you is going to have to struggle. You can both be successful and thrive. It all comes down to your mentality! One person doesn't have to lose so the other person wins.

The attraction of money doesn't have to do with your ability to earn it. It only has to do with your wanting and believing you of your worthiness to receive it.
–Abraham Hicks

Something important that I learned about money years ago from Robert Kiyosaki, the author of *Rich Dad, Poor Dad,* was that you have to respect money. To me respecting money meant appreciating it, understanding its value, and having fun spending it rather than feeling guilty spending it. For years I would feel guilty when I would purchase items, I thought I really didn't need the item and the purchase didn't feel fun. Well, let's face it, we really don't need a majority of what we buy. This is something I learned while sheltering in place during the pandemic. In fact, I realized that we actually need very little; however, that doesn't mean we can't buy stuff because we want it. I learned that when I do buy something because I want it I am investing in our economy, I am supporting another business, I am supporting a family and that feels much better than feeling guilty for spending on items I believe I don't need.

Along with the respect of money comes smart spending. Are we using retail therapy to feel good about ourselves or to keep up with the Joneses? We also must look at the intention behind why we are spending our money. If you are spending money to buy your worth there will never be enough money to buy you and you will end up feeling depleted, defeated, and broke. Yes, money is fabulous and it can provide us with freedom and security; however, it doesn't define us and it can't no matter how you spin it buy us happiness or our self-worth. When we stand tall and confident in our self-worth, happiness and money flow. I know, this sounds counterintuitive because society has ingrained in us that happiness and our worth come after we have made all this money, but that's more bullshit.

Have you ever noticed that when you do need money, it just happens to show up and that when it comes to what you need you really are never without for long? There have been many times in my young life when I was BROKE AS A JOKE! Yet somehow the money always showed up from somewhere. A gift, a check in the mail I wasn't excepting, a generous tip. There is no shortage of money in the Universe and it is available to us and flows to us.

When you step into your fabulousness and kick the shit out of those sad, worn-out tired ass stories that have kept you feeling guilty for having, you are going to set an inspiring example for other women to do the same. If they witness you rise you are absolutely supporting them on their journey! Yes, it is great to have incredible examples like Oprah Winfrey, Jennifer Lopez, and Marie Forleo to inspire us and remind us that incredible wealth can be created from humble beginnings. It's even more powerful to have examples of successful, wealthy women in your own circles and communities that inspire others. You, my beautiful friend, can be that woman. You wouldn't be reading these words if there wasn't at least some small thought in your mind about creating that fabulous life, and part of the fabulous life is attracting prosperity. There is absolutely nothing wrong with wanting and desiring money. It doesn't mean that you are greedy, shallow, or stuck-up. It means that you are stepping into and receiving the life of abundance that God intended for you. You are worthy, you are deserving, and abundance is your birthright!

I can share that I have diminished my limiting beliefs around having to bust my ass and work an unreasonable amount of hours to create financial abundance in my life. As I stepped into my worth and created new stories around my "haviness" and money, clients began to flow into my business with more ease and grace. The process of making money wasn't as hard. It was more fun and it took much less time. In addition, money began to flow from different sources I'd never even thought of. My husband and I invested in businesses that provided semi-passive income, I opened a new stream of revenue with my coaching business, and I overcame my fear of risk and made investments I would never have made in the past.

Diminishing my limiting beliefs around money and worthiness hasn't been easy. It has been a process and, as I mentioned earlier, I have noticed that every time I am about to level up in my life and business those beliefs rear their ugly heads again. Like they say, "New level, new devil." What I can share is that each time our core theme beliefs rear their heads, their intensity lessens. As the awareness you have around each belief grows, it becomes easier to reframe and shift into your powerful story.

Sister, if you get anything from this chapter, I want it to be this: YOU ARE WORTHY of all the prosperity and abundance the Universe has to offer. You don't need to earn it or deserve it. It is yours for the taking. Open up yourself to receiving from multiple sources because you are a GODDESS! OWN IT and allow your God-given prosperity to flow to you. Investing in yourself is the greatest investment you can make and provides the greatest level of returns.

Activity

Take fifteen minutes to sit quietly. Write down as many limiting beliefs as you can about money. You probably aren't even consciously aware of all of them. Once you write down as many limiting beliefs as you can, go back and reframe each one to a more empowering belief. Read these new, empowering beliefs out loud over the next twenty-one days.

Example:

I have to work my ass off to make money.

Empowering: When I am grateful for what I already have money flows to me with ease and grace.

I can't afford it.

Empowering: it's not something I am interested in investing in right now.

Chapter Eight

You Want What You Want?
Then Chill Your A** Out and LET GO!

The simple intention to surrender control is all you need to experience miracles.

–Gabby Bernstein

he word surrender sure is loaded. To me, it used to mean waving that white flag, bowing my head in defeat, and slinking off feeling like a total loser. Like the times in wrestling when The Rock had his opponent in a headlock and pinned on the mat. As the crowd roared and cheered him on, the only option his opponent had to catch his breath and save his life was to tap out and surrender.

I know that sounds a bit dramatic but, hey, if you've watched wrestling, it's a scene that plays out over and over. An opponent surrenders and if they don't, it could cost them their life. Is that what surrender means to you – to tap out, give up, and lose to the other person? If that's the case, no wonder you want no part of it.

I'm here to shift the concept of surrender so many of us hold onto. Surrender DOES NOT mean you have to give up or give in. It can actually be a form of acceptance, allowing the Universe to work *with* you, and *for* you. Feels totally counterintuitive, right? I hear you! It took me a minute to wrap my own head around it.

Okay, here we go on the dope journey to embrace the practice of surrender.

Sometimes we get so attached to an outcome or situation that we just can't let it go. This puts us in a place of resistance, a state where we're trying to control the outcome. It's very much like being in a raft that's trying to go down a river filled with garbage and mud. It's hard – if not impossible – to flow through that river because the raft just keeps getting stuck in the crap.

That's exactly what happens to us when we hold on so tight to situations that are frustrating or aren't going our way. We try to force or control it, all the while complaining and focusing on the circumstances, and end up stuck just as surely as that raft.

So what does this have to do with surrender? Everything, my sweet friend, everything! Surrender means seeing the situation for what it is. It's about saying to yourself, "'Okay, in this moment, this shit really sucks. But I acknowledge and accept it, and there's really nothing else for me to do. It's out of my control."

Yes, I hear you – accepting things isn't easy to do! And I wouldn't advocate this if you're trying to accept a situation that places you in danger or where you don't feel safe. If that's the scenario, please get support and get out immediately.

But if you're not in immediate danger, what I invite you to do is find that sweet spot – where you can acknowledge where you are and accept it while letting go of the outcome. In doing so, you stay open to even better possibilities. The Universe has a much better plan for you than you could ever imagine, but by being stubborn and clinging to situations, you are making it difficult for better experiences, possibilities, and opportunities to flow to you.

There will be times when you surrender and the situation doesn't unfold the way you wanted it to. Just know this – when you surrender, accept, and let go, you're allowing the Universe to work for your highest and greatest good. Sometimes what we think is best for us really isn't, and sometimes the outcome is tragic but typically has a higher purpose, though we may never understand it. Yes, that can be so challenging to accept. I absolutely understand and hear you!

Surrender doesn't mean relinquishing your vision of a better tomorrow. It just means to be flexible and to be open. In fact, there is a saying that those who are most successful are the most flexible. I absolutely believe this to be true, AND that we also must be flexible and release the need to be right. By this, I mean the idea in your mind of how things should be. Oftentimes, that image will not transpire exactly the way we envisioned, especially, when there are factors involved that we can't control (like other human beings).

We can control ourselves and how we choose to respond to situations; this is why flexibility is so important and goes hand in hand with surrender. Surrender provides us with the opportunity to be flexible and open to outcomes that we couldn't imagine on our own. Flexibility in surrender opens us up to attract people and situations that can propel us from feeling like we have a hand wrapped around our airway, constricting our breath, to a more relaxed, peaceful feeling you have when you know that the Universe has your back and things will unfold the way they are meant to for your greatest and highest good.

> *Surrender is faith that the power of love can accomplish anything even when you cannot see the outcome.*
>
> **–Deepak Chopra**

Typically, we are in situations and circumstances with others. We are either the teacher or the student. That's why I emphasize the fact that we can't control anyone outside of us but we can control our own actions and responses.

I had a tremendous fear of loss associated with my oldest son. I felt it in my gut whenever he was out and I wasn't able to get a hold of him. When he was home, he stayed mostly in his room, not interacting much with me or others. I felt like I repelled him, and in fact I probably did because of my controlling, fearful energy. Although I didn't express things out loud, my energy towards him was heavy as shit and certainly not something I would have wanted to be around.

Energy is REAL. People respond to our energy and not what we say. One day it was the middle of the afternoon, three p.m. to be exact, and I was worried because I couldn't get a hold of him. Mind you, he was eighteen years old at the time! He hadn't been going out much so I was wondering where the hell he could be, then the anxiety and craziness started in my head. By four he still hadn't answered his phone and my husband and I had to leave in thirty minutes for a school event for our younger son. I was a hot fucking mess. The anxiety within me

swelled to a point I hadn't experienced in MANY YEARS! In
that moment I knew I had to surrender and let go or I was
going to drive myself crazy. I made a decision in that moment
and sat down on my bed, took a deep breath, and started to
Tap (Freedom Emotional Technique), reciting the Hawaiian
healing prayer Ho'oponopono as I tapped. My husband walked in and looked at me like I was INSANE. For fifteen minutes
I sat there taking deep breaths tapping and reciting the prayer.
I slowly started to feel better and I could feel myself releasing
whatever fear and stories that had a grip on me. In those fifteen
minutes intuitive messages started to come to me and I realized
that the fear that had gripped me was learned from my mother.
She had a tremendous fear of losing her oldest son and because
we absorb everything in the world around us, I had imprinted
that same story within myself. In that moment I was more than
ready to surrender and let go of it, and I did so with another
deep breath. Within minutes of the release my son walked in
and I started crying. He told me I was crazy and to get help!
The magical thing is that after the release of the fear my son
started interacting with me much more; he also started going
out and being more active with his friends. So you see, when
we are making an effort to control others in any way (including
energetically) we push them away from us and the relationship
will suffer. When I surrendered and let go, I was no longer in
resistance, which allowed him to feel more comfortable and
invited a better relationship for us both.

We have a natural tendency to be laser-focused on how we
want things to be. It is absolutely great to have a vision that
helps us manifest and create our lives. It's also key to be open
to how you reach the end goal of what you want. It's critical to
be open to how you achieve your goals and how you reach your
vision. Being flexible and open doesn't mean we are passive;

it means we are strategic and understand that there are going to be bumps along the way and those bumps are helping us take a different path that brings us to an even better opportunity. Each step we take leads us to the next step; however, if we are stuck in our ways and refuse to surrender, accept where we are, and let go, we can miss the path of least resistance – and the blessings that come with it.

Part of surrender is acceptance. Acceptance doesn't mean settling, it just means recognizing what we can and cannot control in any given moment. When we resist the now and fight against what is, it really drains our energy. How motivated do you feel when you feel drained? Exactly, not very motivated at all. Our energy is so critical to creating a fun and fabulous life we love.

When we accept where we are, we open ourselves up to more and better possibilities. Plus, when we surrender and accept where we are and our energy flows better, our mind is better able to identify creative solutions to our challenges. I can't stress enough how important it is to be flexible, open-minded, and make an effort to stay present in the NOW.

Years ago, when I first listened to the audiobook of Eckhart Tolle's *The Power of Now*, it really went over my head! My brain just couldn't comprehend the concept. Now practicing staying in the Now helps me surrender with less resistance. We can't change the past, and worrying about the future doesn't serve us. We can create the most impact by staying present in the moment we are currently experiencing. What's so bad in this current moment right this second? Whatever it is, surrendering brings you a step closer to freedom.

When I started my career in staffing the training, what I received was very cut-throat. It was all about the numbers – how many calls you made a day, how many clients visits you made a week, how many candidates you interviewed – the quotas to meet were brutal! They also trained us to keep our eye on the competition and stay on top of what they were doing. So counterproductive, but, hey, I get it. It's the old-school model and it burned us the fuck out!

I worked for someone else before starting my own staffing firm and I followed the training because I was desperate to be successful. My self-worth and identity were tied to my success, so I hit the pavement and those damn phones, killing myself to prove I was worthy. I would also constantly stress about what the competition was doing, which put me in a state of comparison. When we are in comparison, we are judging ourselves and that is self-sabotage. I was far from surrender and in total resistance! EXHAUSTING!

Even after starting my own firm, I held on tightly to the numbers and on staying on top of the competition. Again, that was very exhausting and I began to lose my joy. I really loved assisting corporate clients in finding the right talent for their teams, and I loved finding awesome dream jobs for my candidates. It was fulfilling, but I knew I had to make a shift and surrender the old ways because that hardcore way of selling didn't feel right to me.

I made the decision to run my own race. I stopped caring about what the competition was doing. Focusing on my competition took the focus away from where it should be: on myself and my business success. I also made a decision to focus on nurturing relationships instead of meeting numbers and quotas. I stopped ruminating over the failures, which weren't really failures but learning experiences. I stopped worrying about what could go wrong in the future. I started to breathe into each moment and made an effort to stay present in the Now.

Instead of looking at what I did as sales (because, to be real, staffing is sales – hardcore sales), I started to view it as building relationships. I let go of the idea that I needed to make a hundred calls a day to be successful and instead started focusing on getting to know my clients and candidates on a deeper level. In surrendering and letting go I also kept an open mind that everything would fall into place.

And with that surrender I gained a new passion for my work. I looked forward to going to the office each day again. It was so fulfilling focusing on growing my own staff, finding my clients great talent for their team, and finding my candidates career opportunities that they loved. When I surrendered to the old ways and focused on what I enjoyed doing, business flowed through the door with ease. I just had to show up with intention and focus on what was important to me and that was providing the best personalized service and value to those that I was doing business with. One of my coaches was shocked at my numbers. He couldn't believe how successful I had been with only making the few calls that we did.

Surrender isn't always going to be that straightforward. There are times that surrender can be very difficult, especially when it comes to our personal relationships. We often hold on to them long after they've run their course. We think if we try just a little harder, if we do just a little more it will work out. What we don't realize is that by holding on to what is no longer working we are keeping ourselves from experiencing better and healthier interactions. And we can also invite illness to us because of the stress created in unhealthy relationships. Staying in situations that don't serve us closes the doors to better opportunities. When we are attached to a story we have created in our minds, we don't allow the Universe to bring us possibilities that are better for us.

Surrender and accept that whatever is happening in the moment, the universe is working on your behalf.

–Mastin Kipp

We don't always have to leave relationships to create healthier interactions; we just need to surrender our version of how we would want things to be. Like I mentioned earlier, we can't control others, we can only control what we do and how we respond. Yes, we want what we want, how we want it. But sometimes the other person isn't able to meet us there, intellectually, spiritually, emotionally, or intimately. Yes, we can voice how we feel and come to a compromise and we can surrender, accept where we are in the situation, and give what we want to receive. When we give what we want to receive, we will bring those things into our lives. It may not always be from the person we want it from, but we will attract those very things our way.

Sometimes letting go is a far greater power than defending or hanging on.

–Eckhart Tolle

My surrender muscles were put to the test during the pandemic. I was accustomed to living life a certain way. I would come and go as I please, traveled, ate out, and ran my business differently from most. Now I no longer had control of even the simplest things, and surrendering to that was very challenging. I have yelled, screamed, cussed, cried, and pleaded to God. I allowed myself to feel what I need to feel. The grief, anger, and frustration were real. And as I sat in my rage with my ego, my higher self knew very well that this was a major lesson in surrender for me. I have felt like I was hitting my head against a brick wall asking for answers, but of course that wall had none to give me. The answers were within me, within my surrender to what is and detaching from the outcome.

When I began writing this chapter, we were eight months into the pandemic and I had just gotten notice that we were moving to an even stricter lockdown. I wanted to cry. I allowed myself to feel my emotions and then went into surrender. I had faith and knew without a doubt that this was only temporary. There were better days ahead, and I surrendered to open myself up to the amazing possibilities and opportunities that can come knocking on the door, even during a pandemic. How did I know this? Because I have had to practice so much surrender during the past eight months and each time that was exactly what came knocking on my door.

For more than a year, I continued to surrender, more than at any other time in my life. Each time I felt discouraged I remembered Michael Singer's book. *The Surrender Experiment*, which I highly recommend. Surrender, then surrender some more, and keep surrendering. Surrender goes hand and hand with trust. I without a doubt believe in the process of surrender to manifest and call into our lives the prosperity, freedom, and peace that is our birthright. There hasn't been anything that I have surrendered to that hasn't unfolded in a way that was more gratifying than I anticipated. I don't want to paint a picture of unicorns and roses because I did have to do the work and take consistent action, but I can assure you when we surrender the magical flow of the Universe steps up very quickly to bring us our heart's desires.

Remember, surrender doesn't mean giving up. It means accepting where you are in the moment, letting go of the outcome and the how, and being open to even better possibilities than you could have ever imagined.

Activity

I invite you to do a google search for the Ho'oponopono prayer and EFT (Emotional Freedom Technique). There are hundreds of short great videos on both tools.

Next, identify a situation that has been triggering you and making you feel anxious. Feel the intensity of the situation and give it a number from 0-10 (0 being not that stressful and 10 being very stressful.) Once you identity the intensity of the trigger with a number, sit For fifteen minutes in a quiet place and practice Faster EFT and Ho'Oponopono as you think of the situation. Hold the intention of surrender and be open to the outcome.

Chapter Nine

The Fascinating Power
of Your Imagination!

Imagination is Everything, it is the preview of life's coming attractions.

–Albert Einstein

Have you ever been on your way to dinner in a busy section of town and thought to yourself *Please, God, let there be a parking spot available for me close to the restaurant* and once you pull onto the block where the restaurant is – boom! – there it is a parking spot waiting just for you! Or, on the flip side, have you ever thought, *Omg, I don't want to go to that party because I don't feel like it and it's going to suck …* and you go to the party and it does, indeed, suck? Both are examples of us creating our lives with the use of our thoughts and imagination. This is the Law of Attraction in action. I call it MAGIC because at times it really feels incredibly magical.

I also like using the term the "Principles of the Universe." Our ancestors and even stories that are found in all the books on religion and spirituality talk about the principles of the universe, even if they don't call them that. Whatever terms we use, I believe in them one hundred percent, and I have had thousands of experiences that confirm that these principles are law.

I believe we create the lives we live, even if they aren't what we want them to be. We created them based on our unconscious beliefs, our conditioning, and stories we tell ourselves – which, as you now know, are mostly false! Now, does unexpected shit happen to us? Absofuckingloulty! There will be things that happen that we can't explain and can't believe and are no fault of our own. That's part of the bigger picture of faith and understanding. However, for the most part, we have a hand in what we call into our lives.

Enjoy the adventure and where you are in the story called your life, because you are exactly where you need to be. The shit we don't want is a contrast to what we do want and that contrast is a gift. We can't be in the rose garden of life every minute of every day. We need the ebbs and flows of life. The ying and the yang. It is necessary for us to gain clarity of what we do want and what we don't want. We might believe we want things a certain way; however, when we get it we realize it's not really what we want and in that contrast we gain clarity. As we learn, grow, and expand, what we thought we wanted changes, and that is one hundred percent okay. It is courageous to be true to yourself and make the necessary pivots, regardless of what you committed to earlier on your path. Be fluid and allow yourself grace as you navigate the journey. There are going to be times we really don't know what the fuck we want and that's totally okay too. Allow yourself to just BE. Allow yourself the pauses. Allow yourself to do nothing. In those moments of nothingness, the clarity will kick in at the precise moment you are ready to take the next steps toward your desires. The desire can be as simple as I want to feel good.

We are constantly creating, even if we don't realize it. So if we are constantly creating and we don't realize it, why not get aware and start taking steps to create what we actually want instead of what we don't.

Trust that you know what is best for you. If you are in conflict about a situation, the best thing to do is nothing. Get quiet with yourself. Typically, our answers come when we are in a relaxed state. My answers typically come in the shower or in my early morning meditations.

If you are like me you probably have created what you wanted but the hard way – with grinding hard ass work and by getting hit in the head by what I call the cosmic two-by-fours. Basically, when I keep doing the same shit over and over expecting a different result and then the Universe is like, "Bitch, please! Now that I have sent the lesson to you so many times and disguised in different ways and you're still not getting it, I am going to knock you off the ledge so you finally understand that you can create in a different way."

I don't believe that I can sit on the couch and just think that I want a windfall of money, the perfect partner, or the ideal client and they will come knocking on my door. Can we create with ease and grace? Yes, I believe we can, but creating the life we want does take dedicated action, commitment, and con-sistency. Are there going to be times that money falls into our laps? YES. Are there times we are going to have amazing connections that feel like they came easily? Yes. Are there times that the amazing ideal client will just show up? Yes. BUT if you look back you will realize you had been taking action to attract those things. The action can be as simple as showing up with an open heart and a mind open to possibilities. Creating a fabulous, fun life we love is about our thoughts, emotions, beliefs, actions, and intention – all working together.

Emotion, Intention and Action are what propel the creation. Before we create, we must absolutely believe without a doubt that we can — not just say we can while having that little lingering doubt in our mind. When we believe, everything in the Universe will conspire to get us what we want. If we say we can't or if we boast that we can and inside we don't believe for a minute, guess what? We can have all the tools, resources, and opportunities brought to us on a silver platter and we still will not be successful in creating. Remember, I am not here to paint you a perfect picture — I am here to be real with you about the effort, commitment, and consistency you need to create the fabulous life you love.

Also remember the pesky distorted beliefs hidden deep down in our subconscious mind. To create the life we love, we must dig deep into our soul. When we tell ourselves those false narratives often enough, we begin to believe them as truth when in reality it's a bunch of crap! Most of the time we are our own worst enemy! If unconsciously we don't believe that we are worthy or deserving of a life we love, we will stay in the hamster wheel we have been trying so hard to get off. You are thinking, *Of course I believe I deserve to have the life I love.* If so, why are you still dabbling in mediocre? Why are you feeling like you aren't able to have, do, and be all that you desire? For a moment, think about one area of your life that you want to change. Once you identify the part of your life that you want to change ask yourself, "What's stopping me?" I am almost certain that there is going to be a false story you are telling yourself. Excuses are lies you are telling yourself! If you really wanted it bad enough you would find a way. Oftentimes your *why* doesn't mean enough to move you into action, or you are just too comfortable and don't really care enough to put in the sincere effort. Typically, fear is what holds us back from putting in the effort.

What you think you become. What you feel you attract. What you imagine you create.

–Buddha

The good news is that even with these hidden irrational thoughts, we can still start creating abundance by applying the laws of the universe to our everyday lives. As you begin to practice these principles you will raise your vibration and as you raise your vibration you will begin receiving messages from within your soul. We really do have all of the answers we need within us.

Here's a scenario you might find helpful. Have you ever been taking a shower, enjoying the feel of the water on your face and feeling so relaxed, and get a great idea or remember something you had forgotten? When we raise our vibration, we become more open to hearing the messages that are within us. The messages about your limiting beliefs will start to sprout up and you will begin to question the false stories you have been telling yourself all these years. Also, you will begin to start seeing examples that prove the story that you believe so strongly is FALSE! The mind is sneaky – it will provide us with examples to affirm our beliefs. Once you realize your story is twisted you will continue to receive information to validate its absurdity. On the flipside, prior to receiving the false evidence, your mind searched for evidence that was validating your bogus story! Crazy, right? It's TRUTH!

Here are some of the principles that I have committed to in order to create fabulous:

What you appreciate, appreciates. Creating a fabulous life we love starts with appreciating the life we have. YUP! Seems counterintuitive, right! You might be asking yourself, *How can I appreciate a stressful life, where I am running like a hamster in the hamster wheel every day and I just can't seem to catch my breath. I am exhausted and don't have energy to think ... what can I appreciate?*

By appreciating what we have, we open ourselves up to attract more and better. During the pandemic, I was forced to learn how to appreciate even the smallest of things we typically take for granted, right down to the air we breathe! Here in Northern California where I live, we experienced the worst fires in state history. As a result, we woke up one morning to what looked like the apocalypse. It was dark for nearly two days straight. Ash was falling on our cars and the air was very unhealthy. We couldn't even go outside. The sky was an eerie orange color. So, as you can imagine, I started appreciating the sun, the clean air, our safety, and electricity. Things that I had taken for granted because the sun, fresh air, and electricity are a given, right? Well, they weren't then, and it taught me to always appreciate these simple "givens" of life.

Even if you are in a challenging time in life, I promise you there is so much to appreciate. Start writing a list of what you appreciate and you will begin immediately attracting more of it.

The same holds true for all that drama that you keep yourself stuck in. All that complaining, blaming, and negativity is only going to bring you more complaining, drama, and negativity. We are a magnet to the exact thing we focus on.

Energy is REAL! When we are in the energy of negativity our vibe radiates that crap. And, like a magnet, we start drawing towards us even more of the same shit. Also, because we have been focusing on and participating in the complaining, drama, and negativity for so long it becomes habitual behavior. The good news is that we can change our negative habitual ways because of a scientific principle called neuroplasticity. Simply put, neuroplasticity is the brain's ability to adapt and form new pathways and connections.

Neuroplasticity gives you the chance to change the way you think, and powerful positive affirmations can help you make that change.

Typically situations and people you are dealing with right now are in direct proportion to what you are thinking and how you are feeling within yourself. We are a mirror of our outside world. I was mortified when I discovered this principle. Like, *Damn, I must really feel like shit about myself because I attracted some shitty people, situations, and interactions.* But here is the thing…it wasn't my fault. It was part of my conditioning. I didn't know any better. I was absorbing the behavior that surrounded me and believing it was "normal." Once I discovered the Principles of the Universe and slowly begin incorporating them into my life, things really began to transform. The people, situations, and interactions I experienced changed from a consistent pain in the ass to consistently good and great. I used to crave love and now my life is overflowing with love – all because I turned inward and began loving myself. That love radiated out as an energy vibration and instead of attracting the negativity I had been attracting, I began attracting love.

To be on the real tip, there are times (though rare, these days) when my mind slips to the habitual thought of "I have no one." Now, I immediately remind myself, "Um, no! That's an old, played-out record, and I turn that tune off and reframe to, "I am so blessed that I have so many loving people in my life."

What you give, you receive back. Many of us have been conditioned to have expectations from others to meet our needs. We want them to be loving, kind, generous, giving, respectful, attentive, and present. We want to be heard and seen. There is nothing wrong to have the desire to want those things. They help us feel connected, and our greatest desire as humans is to feel connected to others.

We would have a powerful and different type of world if most people showed up loving, kind, generous, giving, respectful, and attentive. Where we trip up is here: we expect others to show up this way with us, but we have to show up in those ways to receive those things from others. Most importantly we need to show up that way with ourselves. We are a mirror of what we are attracting. Girl, if you show up salty and prickly you are going to get salty and prickly right back. Even if you show up with a smile, your energy won't hide your saltiness!

> *Whatever is going on in your mind*
> *is what you are attracting.*
>
> **–Rhonda Byrne**

Yes, life gets tough and we slip into our funks. I know when I was knee-deep in my stress although I showed up smiling, but deep inside I was feeling angry, stressed, bitter, and resentful. So, what do you think I was attracting? Yup, other angry, stressed, resentful and bitter people and situations. NOT FUN!

Yes, I was loving and I wasn't hurting anyone, but what I attracted matched my internal energy.

Give yourself love, respect, generosity, and kindness, and you will naturally be loving, generous, and kind to others; then, as the law states, you will attract loving, kind, generous, and joyful interactions.

At this point in my life it is rare that I directly encounter an angry or bitter interaction. Not saying that it doesn't happen, but it really is rare. I am an energy snob; I really don't enjoy giving my power away; however, if I need to vent and explode I absolutely give myself the permission to do so. All of our emotions are healthy. Our emotions are telling us something. Anger is telling us something is out of alignment for us. It is an indicator that a change needs to be made. Typically, when I do encounter someone angry or bitter, I get curious as to what they may be going through and I feel compassion for them.

Yes, our thoughts are very powerful! When we marry our thoughts with our emotions, the results are astounding!

Okay, now you get to be a kid again! One of the most fun and powerful strategies to creating is using your imagination to visualize what you want. The scientific research bears this out. We simulate the same brain region when we visualize doing something as when we are actually doing it. Experimental and clinical psychologists have proved beyond a shadow of doubt that the human nervous system can't tell the difference between an actual experience and an experience imagined vividly and in detail. WHAT?! Plus, everything that was ever created started in someone's imagination. Imagine that! (Yes, pun intended!)

Yes, girl! Start having fun visualizing what you want! Here is another little secret: while you are visualizing what you want, feel it like it's happening; (add the emotions you want to feel). When we couple emotion with visualization it is a phenomenal combination. You are sending a first-class message to the Universe. Remember, the Universe responds to the energy you are putting out. Now your thoughts are working in tandem with your emotions. If you are visualizing what you want but you don't feel good about it or there is a doubt, you are out of alignment and you will not attract what you want. You have to be certain that what you want is yours. You need to believe with certainty that you will attract the people, situations, prosperity, and possibilities that you want to create the life of your dreams.

If there is any doubt or something is really not meant to be, the Universe will not allow the situation to manifest. See, the Universe always has our back. Sometimes what we are visualizing and feeling into isn't what the Universe has in mind; it has something even better in mind that is beyond our imagination. So visualize what you want and be open to even better possibilities that are beyond your wildest dreams.

I have connected with many women who have created incredible lives. Once we start talking, we realize we have created lives that are even better than the lives we imagined. #TRUTH I didn't imagine that before the age of fifty I would be doing work I love for fun, feeling fulfilled, giving back, and helping other women do the same! I never imagined that I would experience the level of joy that I have or be working and collaborating with the wonderful people I have met. I also know there is more and better ahead that exceeds my wildest imagination. I continue to visualize and feel into what I want and the Universe continues to surprise me in ways that keep me in awe.

Once you make a decision, the Universe conspires to make it happen.

–Ralph Waldo Emerson

Again ... we have a choice! Why choose mediocre when you can choose FUN, FIERCE, and FABULOUS! Girl, you would not still be here reading this if you don't have that voice inside you telling you there is more to life for you!

I have had the gift and pleasure of witnessing so many clients and loved ones manifest remarkable situations from utilizing the Principles. I am going to share one of my favorite stories. She was a single mother and had been single for many years because her focus was on raising her young son and committing to her career. There came a point when we were working together when she felt it was time to attract love and sexiness into her life. She was a bit jaded because all of the past romantic relationships she had were not positive experiences. She was constantly getting crumbs, giving more than she was receiving, and she really never felt seen or appreciated as a woman. Together we began unraveling some of the false stories she had hidden deep down in her unconscious. One of the stories was there are no good men out there. "They are all losers!" she said. Now, is that true? Absolutely not, and we came up with examples of strong, solid men she knew. That was another example of a false narrative keeping us safe. It was keeping her safe from hurt and disappointment; however, she no longer needed that fictional story because she was in a place in her life where she had been doing the work, which made her wiser and more aware. Next, I asked her to write down all the qualities she wanted in a romantic partner. I told her, "Go 'balls to the wall,' sister. List everything you want because you are worthy of an amazing partner and more." We actually had a blast with this activity. Then I told her that over the next thirty days she should really imagine this man was in her life. "Feel into it. What does it feel like to be on a date with him? What is that experience like?"

Once she created her list, she opened herself up further by going out more and joining a dating site. Over the course of a few months she met several great fun men and some that were not so great! Those experiences helped her gather information and refine what she did and didn't want. She also learned how to enjoy the feminine part of her and it helped her start to learn how to receive from the opposite sex. She was having a great time exploring dating in an entirely different way. I will never forget one session with her. I could tell something was different as soon as she walked into the office. Her energy was on fire! When I said as much, she told me she had met a man who met her checklist of wants to the tee! Even I was floored! I was so inspired by her manifestation! She inspired me and reminded me how we are all incredible powerful manifesters and we can do, be, and have whatever we set our mind to.

There are days when I still can't believe how I have created the incredible life that I live. Is my life perfect? Of course not. As long as we are breathing, we will be faced with challenges. As long as we are living and breathing, there is always room to learn, grow, and expand spiritually, and challenges help us do that. When we are too comfortable, we get stagnant and BORED. Through the Laws of the Universe, I have learned to create lemonade out of lemons and appreciate the imperfections of life because they make us who we are. Based on my therapist's feedback when she met me at nineteen my story should have turned out a very different way. Now, was it easy to get where I am today? Absolutely not; however, it absolutely was worth the effort and work I invested in my healing and growth.

Girl, I want you to KNOW that YOU ARE a MASTER MANIFESTOR! So why not start creating that magical fabulous life you really love! Let's have some fun.

Activity

Today I am inviting you to play a fun and fabulous game with your imagination. As I young kid I used to play this game all the time to escape reality. Little did I know I was helping create the life I live now.

Grab your notebook. Sit in a quiet place. Light your candle. Pick one thing that you would like to manifest in your life. Start writing down all the things you want. If you want to create a fabulous business, write down how you would want that business to look and what type of clients you would like to attract. (Tip: I have also used the "notepad" app on my iPhone to do this exercise, and I still do this all the time!) Dream big, girl! Go balls to the wall! MOST IMPORT-ANTLY, BELIEVE with unwavering certainty that the dream is yours! It is your right to have it; you don't need to deserve it! Remember, the Universe will bring you manifestations that are even greater than what you imagined!

Once you have written your list, take a deep breath, put your hands on your heart, and imagine what it would feel like if you already had it. Feel into it. What emotions would you feel? Excitement, Joy, Happiness, Baddassness … continue to feel into it for three minutes, then take another deep breath and say these words: "And so it is!"

Now for the next twenty-two days, take just five minutes to review your list and feel into it like it's already happened. You can work on more than one manifestation at a time if you like; just create a different list and spend the five minutes imagining that at a different time of the day! Happy Creating, my love!

Chapter Ten

Would You Take a Road Trip Without Your GPS?

It's our intention. Our intention is everything.
Nothing happens on this planet without it. Not one
single thing has ever been accomplished
without intention.

–Jim Carrey

ave you ever wanted something so bad that you can feel it in your bones? You just keep thinking about it and focusing on it and then you – voila! – it happens and it's yours. That is, you set an intention to call into your life what you want.

Our intentions are very powerful. We create our lives through intentions and we don't even realize it. Unfortunately, many of us unconsciously create through fearful and lack-based intentions. What we think is picked up by the Universe, and it's the Universe's job to bring us what we put out there. Whoever said, "Be careful what you wish for!" wasn't kidding!

For years, my core story was, "I always get rejected," and – you guessed it – I experienced a tremendous amount of rejection in certain areas of my life. Why? Because that was the message I was putting out into the Universe. Remember, per universal law energy flows where intention goes.

We all emit an energy frequency. When we are in a low-energy frequency (i.e., a state of lack or fear) that is the energy we put out to the universe, which then delivers experiences matching that frequency. If you have been creating from a place of fear and lack, it's now time to create from a place of faith and love!

Now, you can achieve your desires creating from a place of fear, but it's exhausting and you constantly feel like you're chasing your tail. You take a few steps forward and several steps back.

Think of your intention as your internal GPS. Now, I don't know about you but I sure as hell wouldn't get in my car to go on a road trip without directions. I'd be completely lost, going in circles with my head spinning. That's what GPS is for. We enter our destination and the GPS guides us to our intended arrival. With the guidance of the GPS, we have a clear idea of where we are going and we typically successfully reach our destination with ease. Sure, there can be traffic that slows us down, but we get there much easier when we can clearly see the road ahead.

Where do you want to be? Who do you want to be? What do you want to do? What do you want to have? Frankly, the how of your intention isn't as important as your why. Behind everything we want to do, be, or have is a deeper WHY.

Let's say, for example, that your intention is to find a new job. And let's say your why is that your boss isn't nice to you and you want a better one. Why do you want a better boss? So you can look forward to going to work. Why do you want to look forward to going to work? Because it feels good. One hundred percent of the time the why behind our intention is we want to feel better than we feel in the present moment. Even the intention to get the parking spot at the front of the restaurant will make you feel excited because you won't have to walk far or waste time driving around in circles.

If, per universal law, we can be, do, and have whatever we want, why not start setting the intention and focus on what we do want instead of what we don't? It is important to get clear on your why because you may be able to achieve your why and feel good with a completely different intention than you originally had in mind.

Remember in our example that you want to change jobs because you aren't feeling good about the interactions with your boss. Here's the thing: there are lessons to be found in our most challenging interactions. If you leave one job and go to the next without having learned the lesson, you will continue to face the same challenges. Since your real desire is to feel good at work, start by setting that as your intention. As I mentioned previously, one way that we can feel good is by practicing appreciation for the current situation. What is something that you appreciate, even in the challenge? Once you set the intention to feel better you will gain clarity around exactly what you do want and what you don't want.

As you set the intention to feel better and appreciate the lesson in the challenge you notice something interesting happens! Your boss, the one making your life miserable, gets moved to another department and you get a new boss you love. You really didn't need a new job in that moment, you just needed to shift your intention to achieve your why of feeling good now. It isn't always going to be that easy, but I have heard so many stories like that, and have experienced my own similar manifestations as well.

*Never underestimate the power of intention. Your
thoughts, your words…They are the keys
to your future.*

–Wayne Dyer

In my early twenties I had a boss who was horrific! She lied, manipulated, and bullied her way around the office. The other employees felt exactly the way I did. We cringed being around her. I remained polite and kind and took her shit because at that point in my career I didn't know any better. There were days I cried the whole drive home. I prayed and asked God to please help me make her leave. You can't imagine how happy I was when I heard she accepted an opportunity with our competitor and was leaving the company! HALLELUJAH! By praying to have her removed from my life I had put that intention out there and didn't even realize it! Again, that's not always going to be the case but I sure love that story!

Now that you are aware of the power of intention-setting, you can take your life in your hands and begin consciously setting intentions that will benefit you. Oftentimes our unconscious intentions may not benefit us. My intention to eat the second slice of cake really isn't going to benefit me. The reason I want to eat that second slice of cake is it will feel good in the moment and I will get a dopamine rush; however, within minutes I will have a sugar crash and feel lethargic and crappy. In other words, my intention to feel good has backfired. Is there another intention that you can consciously set to provide you with that dopamine rush? Instead of eating the second slice of cake, why not call your best friend and have a conversation that makes you feel good?

Just like the GPS will get us to our destination quicker, so will the Universe when we have clarity and intention.

One tool I have found extraordinary is attaching emotion to my intention-setting. It's what Abraham Hicks calls "segment intending." Throughout the day I set micro intentions. I start in the morning by setting the intention for how I would like the day to unfold. I imagine how I want to feel and visualize myself feeling the emotion. I love having fun and connecting with people. Most mornings I set the intention to have a fun day where I feel connected. I literally take a few minutes to feel joy because when I'm having fun, I feel joyful and when I feel connected I feel fulfilled. I don't know exactly how I am going to bring the fun and connection in and that's okay – the Universe will provide the how. Also, when we are open to the outcome we allow miracles to surprise and awe us!

As you practice segment intending and become consistent with it the Universe is going to respond in a beautiful and delightful way. It's like the compound effect, you will reap tremendous rewards from small seemingly insignificant actions. What you don't realize is that it's those small, seemingly insignificant actions we commit to each day that create the monumental opportunities in our lives. The more you receive what you have intended, the more you realize that IT IS LAW! Having those examples to refer back to helps rewire your brain to operate from this truth. Having that tool in your treasure chest is like Popeye's spinach! It will become another one of your superpowers.

The Universe LOVES you! It wants to shower you with all of your dreams and desires. How good do you feel when you give to another? Exactly! The universe wants to give you everything you desire because it's in vibrational alignment with the ultimate intention and that is the vibration of LOVE.

When your intention is clear, so is the way.

–Alan H. Cohen

I would like to share another example of segment-intending. When I have a meeting that I feel nervous about, I take a moment to set the intention for the meeting. It may go something like this. I close my eyes and conjure the feeling that I want to feel. In this case I want to feel confident, I want to communicate clearly, and I want to provide value. I spend literally sixty seconds visualizing myself in a confident state, clearly articulating what I would like to communicate and then I visualize my audience inspired because they gained value from their interaction with me. Eight times out of ten I walk away from my meeting feeling even better than anticipated. The times I walk away wobbly I know it's because I was wobbly going in. Hey, I can take accountability for my shit!

Setting intentions takes commitment and consistency, but before you know it, it will become habit. As you get better at setting intentions you take control of the GPS and you will begin noticing the changes that begin to take place in your life. The more you set feel-good, positive intentions, the more feel-good and positive interactions, possibilities, and opportunities you will attract.

Setting intentions will also help you move forward with your aspirations and desires. I used to set goals but as I moved forward in my spiritual journey, I realized that the word "goal" wasn't resonating with me anymore. While working in my staffing business it was all about setting goals and I did meet many of the goals I set; however, when I didn't meet the goal it felt like shit. So I have learned to use intentions in place of goals. The intention is to feel fulfilled, help others, attract abundance doing it, and learn from the experiences I am having. From there I set smaller intentions. For example, I would meet an amazing candidate and set the intention of attracting an incredible opportunity for them. That fulfilled me and created abundance in the business. My recruiting coach Mike would ask me, "Do you really have close to a one-to-one placement ratio?" He didn't believe that I was able to send one candidate out to interview and close the placement. To be transparent, I was doing this before I really knew about the universal laws. That just goes to show how we are constantly creating.

I want to share a funny story about my son Raymond and an intention he set without even realizing it. One Saturday morning, he didn't want to go to his rugby game, which was two hours away. He and I fought all morning; I was adamant about him going and he was adamant about staying home and enjoying his time gaming online with friends. He yelled that he hoped he broke his back in the game. I yelled back at him that I would NOT take care of him if he did. I told him to be ready to go once I got back from my hot yoga class. I was going to drop him off where the players were meeting for the two-hour drive. I got back from class, picked him up against his will, and went to the pick-up point, and – OMG! – there was no one there! His intention not to go to the game was unfolding, but my controlling ass was like, *Oh, hell no. I am going to drive you two hours away in my soaking wet after-hot-yoga nasty clothes and ruin my day if I have to.* I bitched the two hours there, then he ran out of the car to meet his team. I stayed away from everyone and walked to the end of the field because I was a hot mess in my now cold, sticky clothes. Within ten minutes of the game starting there was a kid laid out flat on the floor. My heart sank and I started running toward the field. I had a feeling I knew who the kid was. As I got closer to the field I noticed the kid had blood rushing down his face and the coaches were wrapping his head. As I got closer the kid was Raymond. Thank Goodness he was okay! He got up and started walking toward me. I said to him, "You know you manifested getting out of playing in the game. Thank God you didn't really hurt yourself. Now get in the car and let's go get some pizza." That was a two-fold lesson. When someone sets an intention and has an unwavering commitment to it watch out AND we/I can't control the will of another person. It will backfire on us.

A component of setting intentions is also relinquishing control. YES, much easier said than done. There have been instances where I was very stubborn. I wanted what I wanted when I wanted it and I just kept hammering away to get it. What I didn't realize is that attachment to what I wanted was a form of control and resistance. Finally, when I just gave up because I had no more energy to "fight," then – boom! – I would get what I wanted. Now, it didn't always show up in the way I had envisioned but it would manifest. It's in the letting go that we receive. When we give up the struggle and trust the Universe, we will attract our desires and, girl, let me tell you: what the Universe has in mind for us typically trumps our vision of what we imagined. (#truth!)

In working with and speaking to hundreds of women I have discovered a sneaky and almost universal myth that manifesting it has to be hard. That goes back to the conditioning that we have to bust our asses to make it. Now, are we going to put some bust-ass action into building what we want? For sure, because bust ass-action can be so fun and motivating, however, when it is driven by fear and lack, watch out. It will, more often than not, be difficult, and you may even crash and burn. We do this because we believe that if it was easy, we wouldn't be worthy or good enough. That, my friend, is COMPLETE RUBBISH! Now, must we take inspired action – at times – massive action? YES! Are there times when we are going to hustle and grind? YES! Is it a 24/7 hustle and grind? NO! Please hear me when I say this: how hard you work and how many hours you put into DOING doesn't equal your worth. YOU ARE ALREADY WORTHY, NO MATTER WHAT!

For me, life has turned into a game. Each day I gather information to learn what I want. It's okay if your desires and intentions change. You are gathering information as you go and you are the author of your life story; you get to choose how you want to write the story and what you want to attract. Then set the intention and don't be so hard on yourself. Chill out, BE, and have FUN. Surrender to the outcome. The intention will manifest in much easier ways.

Our experiences allow us to keep redefining and refining what we want. We can't control circumstances outside of us; however, when we surrender controlling those circumstances and put the spotlight on what we desire, the Universe has a funny way of moving those circumstances out of our way or softening the circumstances.

When we approach life only from a place of action, we are missing out on the potency of feminine divine energy that allows us to create from a place of flow as opposed to a place of survival and hustle. Just put your intention out there and don't get caught up in the details. If you have imagined it, it's yours for the taking.

An excellent strategy to help you create magic is to begin each morning with an intention-setting ritual, even if it's just taking five minutes to breathe into how you want the day to unfold.

We really underestimate the power of our mind. It can fuck us up and it can propel us into our limitless potential. Through setting intentions, we are communicating with Source Energy and asking for what we want. Remember, ask and you shall receive. That is why it is very important to be careful about what you ask for.

Believe that you already have what you desire and that will set the process of receiving into motion. Give thanks for the intention like it has already happened. This sends a message to the Universe that you are ready to receive, and it will start lining up the information and situations you need to move toward your desire.

When I had the nagging desire to pursue my certification as a success coach, I had absolutely no idea where to start. One afternoon, while I was doing research for my business, an advertisement for a life coach popped up. I had been in therapy for over twenty years and had a handful of business coaches, but I had never hired a life coach. My intuition kicked in and whispered to me, *Call her.* Valerie Smedley Harris was such an incredible and beautiful human being, and what she provided me in our time together was priceless. The Universe brought her to my attention because I set the intention. From there the other pieces of the intention puzzle began to come together. I asked Valerie where she had received her schooling, and she had great feedback about the program she attended. I checked into the program and made the decision to pursue their life coaching certification.

Other pieces of the intention puzzle began to fall into place in a very whimsical way. Valerie had suggested I do a search for life coaches in my local area, just to get an idea and get in the momentum of attracting my professional tribe. I hopped on Linkedin and one person who came up was Mark Shihadeh. I was like, "Hey, my mother's side of the family has that last name." (He even looked like my family!) I was excited that there may be someone in my community that I could touch base with and ask questions about this new adventure I was embarking on.

I was eager and excited to get to my first life coaching class that Friday afternoon. My instructor Luke Benoit was awesome! He was a recovering drug addict who now coached young people in recovery, and his stories of transformation were so inspiring and motivating. The next day Luke mentioned that he was bringing in one of his colleagues to speak with us that afternoon. Can you guess who his colleague was? Mark Shihadeh! I WAS FLOORED! It was an incredible synchronicity (by the way nothing is a coincidence! Synchronicities are the Universe's way of lining up the pieces of the puzzle to help us step into our intentions). I spent most of the presentation in shock, thinking, *REALLY? This shit is so cool, you can't make it up.* After Mark finished his presentation, I bolted out of my chair and rushed to him, saying, "Hi, I am Grace Redman and we are cousins." He looked at me like I was crazy but once I explained we both laughed. The Universe knows how to line up the right situations for us to help move us forward. Mark would later become one of my mentors who really helped me elevate my game and moved me closer to unleashing my creative potential as a coach.

What I hadn't realized was that over the last three decades I had been setting both unconscious and conscious intentions to move me toward my career as a success coach. I didn't even realize I had the intention of helping others brewing in my soul. In writing this, I just had a memory pop up (I love how Spirit speaks with us!) When I first met my husband, he took me to visit one of his very wise friends. His friend asked me what I wanted to do with my life. I remember I told him I wanted to help other women. He asked me how, and I said I really didn't know. It took twenty years for the how to unfold. The main thing was I had a desire, an intention, and the rest flowed into my life in divine timing.

It's just a matter of time before you experience the manifestation of your desires and intention. Do keep this in mind: your desires will manifest based on your preparedness to receive. When I was twenty-six years old I was in no way ready to step into that role because I first needed to undergo my own healing and transformation.

Also fascinating is that I had been journaling since I was a teenager, writing out my goals and desires. Recently I pulled out some of my journals from more than a decade ago and was floored because I achieved ninety percent of the goals I wrote out. I also believed the affirmations I had written out, even though I'd had difficulty believing them at that time.

I am not wearing rose-colored glasses or here to sell you a farfetched dream. Living the fabulous life doesn't mean everything just gets handed to you on a silver platter. There are going to be things you desire that just don't come into your life fast enough. They say patience is a virtue for a reason. We are exactly where we need to be every step of the way on this journey. We can't get moved from kindergarten to senior year in high school overnight. Our journey in this life is similar – each step of the way we gain more knowledge and awareness that helps move us into the next level of our fabulous. Our manifestations unfold at the pace at which the Universe feels we are ready. And yes, we can absolutely own our fabulous every step of the way. It really isn't about arriving; it's about enjoying every step of the adventure along the way. It's like adding amazing new nuggets of experience to your treasure chest.

I LOVE YOU! I want you to KNOW without a doubt that you can greet your desires and passions with enthusiasm in this lifetime. Start consciously practicing setting your intentions and the manifestations will begin to mystically appear. Have fun adding new experiences and nuggets of wisdom to your treasure chest along the way.

Activity

Start each morning this week with a five-minute intention-setting practice. When you wake up, take a moment to visualize yourself moving through your day and feel the emotion of what you want to experience. If you have to be in a situation that you aren't that comfortable with, imagine the situation going very well and you walking away from it feeling empowered.

Chapter Eleven

No Matter What, Trust All Is Well!

God puts rainbows in the clouds so that each of us – in the dreariest and most dreaded moments – can see a possibility of hope.

–Maya Angelou

I didn't grow up in a particularly religious home. My father was Antiochian Orthodox and, according to custom, my mother, who was Catholic, would get married in the Orthodox church. That said, my father was never big on religion so we rarely went to church unless it was a holiday or my grandparents took me. I fondly remember Palm Sundays. A few days before, Dad would bring home these huge palms and an abundance of beautiful carnations and we would decorate our palms with the carnations for the Palm Sunday procession around the church. All the families dressed up in their Sunday best and made the procession while hearing the beautiful chanting, smelling the distinct smell of the incense in the air, and being mesmerized by the colors of the beautiful stained-glass pictures of all the saints.

I loved our church, St. Nicholas. It was beautiful, with white marble floors, those incredibly ornate stained-glass icons, and an even more ornate, spectacular ceiling. On a sunny day the sun would flood through the windows and there would be orbs around the entire church. At that time I had no idea what an orb was. I just knew I felt so safe and at peace when I was sitting in the pew. Our priest, Father Gregory, was an amazing, charismatic, wise and an incredible speaker. He was motivating and inspiring. He spoke with conviction. He spoke in a way that the young, the old, the religious, and the not-so-religious would be moved by his words. I absolutely loved hearing Father Gregory preach as a young girl. He was my first experience with a motivational speaker and, years later, he married me and my husband. St. Nicholas was also the church where my two children were baptized.

To this day I feel a sense of overwhelming peace when stepping into most spiritual dwellings. I can almost always feel the magnificence of our powerful Creator, our higher power, God, The Universe, Our Creator, Spirit, or whatever word you feel resonates with you that describes that all-knowing energy frequency that embodies us all.

I was on a trip to Sedona with my soul sisters one year and they took me to visit the Chapel of the Holy Cross. I had heard them talk about it, but what awaited me was far more magnificent than I could ever have imagined. The moment I walked into the tiny space I gasped with awe. There was an enormous statue of Jesus facing you as you walked in. My entire body was immediately flooded with emotion and the tears started rolling down my face. I know in the deepest part of my soul that the overwhelming emotion that just washed over me was my unconditional love and connection to God. It was gratitude for the higher power that I can't see but KNOW WITHOUT A DOUBT is present. I have experienced many of those moments in my lifetime. Feeling that connected to God reminds me that all things are possible and how blessed I have been. Even in my darkest hours, God always carried me.

As I mentioned earlier, I really don't know too much about religion because I never consistently went to church or studied the bible; however, I always knew that I loved God. When I was nine years old, I noticed that the Lutheran Church several blocks away was having a bible study summer camp. Back in those days kids were more independent; we roamed the neighborhood all day and came home when it got dark. Our parents had no cell phones to reach us. So I skipped down to the Lutheran church for summer camp. I remember just walking in that first day and the pastor and staff welcomed me with open arms. There were no questions asked. Immediately I felt at home and safe.

In those two weeks at camp, it felt amazing to be seen, heard, and supported by the camp staff. It was exhilarating to listen to the stories that each teacher shared from the bible. I was fascinated. One day, one of the teachers invited me to share a story about a time I felt close to God. That was such an exciting moment for me. I felt so happy to be invited to share and to be seen. That moment in that circle has stayed with me and inspired me when I become insecure as an adult to show up.

I am very grateful for those experiences early on in my life. I truly believe they helped plant the seed of faith in my heart. Being that my mother was Catholic, she was a big believer in the Virgin Mary and God. My mother lived a very difficult and stressful life, and whenever anyone asked her how she was doing she would always answer, "Nushkurl Allah," which is Arabic for "Thank God." During my challenges I would remember my mother and her faithfulness even during such difficult times.

As I grew into a teenager, I fell into the same distractions many teens do and wasn't as connected to my faith or spirituality. Then, at sixteen, I began experiencing my first bouts of depression. I was very lonely and felt a sense of despair and hopelessness. I didn't feel like I had anyone to talk to. I felt isolated and sad. As I look back on those dark times in my young life, and even though I wasn't nurturing my connection with Spirit I know that Spirit was with me every step of the way. Spirit is always with us every step of the way, regardless of our religious beliefs, or even the complete lack of them.

One poem that resonated for me as a young girl was footprints in the sand.

Here are a few paragraphs from that poem:

"You promised me, Lord, that if I followed you, you would walk with me always. But I have noticed that during the most trying periods of my life there has only been one set of footprints in the sand. Why, when I needed you most, have you not been there for me?

The Lord replied, "The years when you have seen one set of footprints, my child, is when I carried you."

I carried those two powerful paragraphs in my heart for decades as I navigated some of the most difficult times in my life.

One of the most difficult was when I was nineteen. I had gotten myself into some trouble and I had no one I felt safe to talk to. We were taught to wear a mask and show that everything was perfect, even with our closest friends. I was feeling lost, depressed, and alone and didn't know what to do or who to turn to. One night, as I lay in my bed wide awake, stressed, and worried, I began to feel very warm. I noticed an overwhelming sense of peace embody me. My body felt light. I felt a feeling that I had never felt before and suddenly I had an experience I could never erase. A vision of an angel appeared in front of me, hovering above my feet. Thinking back on that moment right now as I write makes me very emotional. I saw beautiful colors surrounding the angel. I do believe it was Mother Mary. Her presence engulfed me and her presence spoke to me. I had an overwhelming knowing that I wasn't alone. Everything would be okay and everything did unfold for me and the solution I needed presented itself.

It was that experience that awakened me to the signs and synchronicities that are greater than us. The signs and synchronicities that we can't make up and that we can't explain. From that moment I began to hear Spirit when it spoke to me. Shortly after that night I stumbled onto an ad in the newspaper for eight-dollar therapy sessions for college students. Seeing that ad wasn't random. Spirit was putting me in the right place at the right time. I had no doubt in my mind that there is an all-knowing power, energy field, Spirit, that is propelling us on our journey. We have that power, that energy field, that knowing within us.

When I was in my early twenties, I began attending Al-Anon. One of the steps I remembered clearly was "Let go and let God." I know with certainty and unwavering faith that when we let go and surrender to God, our higher power, the Universe, everything, NO MATTER WHAT IT IS, will work itself out the way it's meant to, even if it ends in a "loss" or "tragedy." Our losses and tragedies are lessons moving us into our greater self and closer to God.

After almost a year of excruciating undiagnosed pain, at the young age of forty-eight my mother was finally diagnosed with stage-four cancer. I will never forget that moment in the doctor's office. My heart dropped and I knew intuitively the end was near. The fear that swept over me was a fear I had never felt before. That fear was a knowing. Fourteen months later, when I was eight months pregnant with my younger son, I was sitting at my mother's bed side administering morphine to her every couple of hours to help her transition from her body and into her eternal spirit. To say it was difficult to do that is an understatement. Each time I had to fill the syringe and shoot the liquid through her lips that were still pink and beautiful with life, I felt like a knife was plunging through my heart. The tears would flood down my face every time. I felt like I was the one killing my mother. In that horrific moment, where was God? I was exhausted, depleted, and afraid my grief was affecting the new life growing inside of me. I was also worried about my other son, then a toddler, who I had hardly seen in days.

My perception was that I had to be the rock for not only my family and extended family, but also for my mother's friends, who were all devastated. This, in addition to a devastation I had never felt in my entire life. The grief was unbearable. I was numb. In shock. How could this happen to me? Looking back, I really don't know how I made it through that night and the days, months, and years that followed. Oh wait, I do know how I made it through: with the grace and mercy of God.

That day when my mother was in her last moments of life our home was filled with our loved ones. There were over fifty people at a time coming in and out. The priests from the Orthodox church and the priests from the Catholic church came to hold vigil with us. The hospice nurse was with me every step of the way with her compassion, kindness, and gentleness. My cousin Rana, who was a nurse, came to support me and comforted me reminding me that I wasn't killing my mother by administering the morphine but helping her have an easier transition. My assistant and team at the office stepped up and handled the business so I could focus on my mother. My husband and mother-in-law were present for our son as I navigated what felt like hell on earth.

Even in that moment when I questioned God and my faith, He didn't leave me. He sent real-life angels one after another to support me. One would think that it's a horrific tragedy to lose your mother this way, and at such a young age; however, as I mentioned earlier even in our losses and tragedies everything unfolds the way it's meant for a greater good, even if we can't see it at the time. And, yes, there are going to be cases where we *never* know what the greater good is. We simply have to trust and believe.

My mother's death was the catalyst that moved me into my deepest healing journey. It was her death that propelled me to commit to breaking generational cycles. It was her death that motivated me to choose me, set boundaries, and step into my power. She was a pivotal character in my life story, and I wouldn't be where I am today without living that chapter, as awful as it was.

Trust yourself and the divine in you. Know that all things are working together to support you living your best life.

–**Lisa Nichols**

I have noticed that the deeper I dive into my triggers and healing my childhood wounds, the more connected I become to Spirit. The more I unwind the ridiculous stories created by my wounds, the closer I get, not only to Spirit, but to my true authentic self. Spirit is within us. We are Spirit. Spirit is pure and unconditional love. I believe we incarnate into this life to heal our wounds and step into unconditional love for ourselves. Love is MAGIC. Love is Spirit. Love Heals. Love Expands. Love is the answer. No, it's not always easy to love but that is our mission to move as close to love as possible. Love is what connects us all. In certain situations, choosing ourselves and disappointing others may not seem like a loving act; however, it is loving when we come from a place of love for ourselves. Remember, if the situation isn't working for us, it isn't working for the other person. Setting the boundary is one of the most loving things we can do.

The Universe is strategic. There is a plan. The closed doors in our lives are part of our destiny. Those closed doors are only detours moving us toward the path that is meant for our good. There are no coincidences, only synchronicities.

That boyfriend that left you brokenhearted was being moved out of the way to make space for the man who would appreciate how amazing you are. No one can stop what is meant for you. Spirit pushes you forward and moves people and situations out of your way and brings the right people and situations into your life for your highest and greatest good. Sometimes we are stubborn and need to keep experiencing those fucked-up moments until finally we get it and we move forward. To keep it real ... yes there are times people don't get it and they stay in the deep dirty mud. They refuse to grab the lifejacket the Universe is throwing to them.

God created us to live abundant, prosperous lives. It is up to us to take the bull by the horns and step into our unwavering faith. We are not always going to understand the events that unfold in our lives and the events that unfold are not always going to seem fair or just. Stay in faith and gratitude. You may not always know the why, just know that there is one and let that be enough.

"Crazy faith" is thoughts and actions that lack reason but trusting fully in what you cannot explicitly prove.

–Mike Todd

As I reflect back on my life, I can see clearly how even the most heartbreaking moments unfolded for my greater good. It's like a domino effect. I struggled with my family. Many in my family were very abusive and toxic. They started rumors about me that were not true and turned people against me. In that moment I felt abandoned, I felt ashamed. I felt like I didn't have a voice, no one was hearing me. It felt unfair and unjust. How could the people that were supposed to love and protect me throw me to the wolves? The fire within me to rise may have never been ignited if I didn't have that experience. Success felt like the best revenge to me. God knew exactly the situation I needed to propel me to make the changes and take the steps to expand into my own gifts and greatness. Today I am grateful for the villains in my story, for, truly, they weren't villains… they were my motivators.

Opposition, betrayal, and tough times are an inevitable part of life, and a strategic part of our growth. Even during those challenges, I promise you the Universe still has your back. I know it is very painful to walk through those moments. You have every right to feel angry and disappointment and to express them. It's even okay to yell and scream; that doesn't make you crazy, it makes you smart for moving emotions out of your body instead of internalizing them. When you have felt the pain you needed to feel and you are ready, step into your Faith and know with certainty that the Universe is working for you and not against you. As if by magic, the doors will open for you and the right opportunities, possibilities, and solutions will show up to move you forward.

I know from experience that when we are in the eye of the storm and experiencing a dark night of the soul it isn't easy to stay in faith … and yet that is exactly what I invite you to do when you fall. Come back to your faith. Trust that all will absolutely work itself out. Hasn't it all worked out for you so far?

There is an incredible story of faith I want to share with you. My friend's husband had an excruciating toothache. They made an emergency appointment to see the dentist, who examined him and delivered the most devasting news you could ever hear. He had a previously undetected deadly infection that had spread into his entire face and he wasn't going to make it. The doctor told my friend to go home and make arrangements. Shocked beyond belief, she said, "There has to be a chance. This can't be the final prognosis." She then asked the doctor to please just give her the chance of survival. The doctor replied, "One percent." My friend took that one percent chance and prayed and reached out to her family and together they held vigil and prayed for the return of her husband's health. She held the vision with unwavering faith that her husband would come home. Being a religious woman, she pulled a verse from the scriptures, Matthew 17:20, which says, "if you have faith as small as a mustard seed, you can say to this mountain, move from here to there and it will move. Nothing will be impossible for you." Thanks to that "mustard seed," her husband is alive and home with them. It wasn't an easy journey. There were many, many dark moments, but her faith always remained strong. Again, I know not all situations will unfold in this way because life happens, but there are also far too many miracles for us to not have faith in a power greater than us.

One of my deeper intentions as I walk this journey called life is to get more consistently connected to Source. You know, that little voice that you hear in your head, that gut feeling that gnaws at you? That's Source speaking with you. Our intuition becomes heightened the closer we get to Source. The messages and synchronicities get stronger and stronger as we release the stories of fear and lack. I am not here to tell you to wear rose-colored glasses; I am here to tell you that there is an incredible power that you can tap into that will be your greatest cheer-leader, your most amazing team member, and your best guide.

Activity

Meditation is getting quiet and listening to the messages that fall in. Prayer is talking and asking for what we want.

Each morning for the next five days, I invite you to sit in meditation for ten minutes. Don't worry about completely silencing your thoughts, just sit quietly and allow them to pass through without engaging with them.

In the evening I invite you to talk to God. Ask Him for support. Ask Him the why's. Just asking is also a form of prayer. Prayer can come in any way shape or form you choose. I talk to God in the car, in the shower, any time of day I feel like it.

After five days, take notice of any changes you have experienced. Take notice of any messages that may have come your way.

I love the signs. I used to get so annoyed when my spiritual friends talked about the signs they saw every day, because I didn't see them as signs. Now I see the signs every day, multiple times a day. The signs for me come in the form of butterflies, dragonflies, feathers, and consecutive numbers such as 111, 222, and 555. Your signs will look different for you. Our Higher Power is always communicating with us. We just need to take the time to pay attention and listen.

Chapter Twelve

Own Your Fabulous Sexy Self!

Beauty begins the moment you decide to be yourself.
–Coco Chanel

I was only four years old when I opened the front door and saw two beautiful queens standing there. Their hair fell long and shiny down their shoulders, their faces were perfectly made up, their lips were painted red, and their clothes made them look like they walked out of a fashion magazine. I've always been fascinated by beauty and sensuality, but that was the first time I was in awe of it. I wanted to be just like my mother and her friends.

They were always dressed to the nines in the most beautiful clothes and flawless makeup. I was mesmerized by glamour and the sex appeal that went hand in hand with it. It was such a magical treat when they would take us with them to an evening party of music and dancing. My eyes would be wide open as I watched them flow in their beauty and elegance. I enjoyed witnessing their laughter and was fascinated by how easily they flirted with the men and women around them. I always felt the magical flow of connection when I was at those parties and witnessing the sensual energy move through the room as I danced along to the mesmerizing beat of Arabic music.

Based on these early experiences, I believed sexy was all about how you looked. Granted, sex itself was a taboo subject, something never to be talked about. Sex before marriage was forbidden and forget about dating ... only bad girls did that. Ironic, because I was also taught to never leave the house without makeup and high heels. I would scream at my mom like a rebel in my late teens and early twenties, "Mom, I am only going to the store, why do I need to put my heals and lipstick on!"

Her answer: "Because you never know who you might run into." This created a story in my head that I was only presentable if I was decked out.

As a teenager I watched evening drama soaps like *Dallas* and *Dynasty* and really wanted to be like the main female characters. They were so strong, so confident, so sexy. They didn't give a fuck about anything and they got whatever they wanted. I wanted to not give a fuck because it felt so heavy to care about what everyone thought about me. It was a suffocating, trapped feeling and I wanted to be free like a bird like the confident women in these shows. I wanted to know how they could live a life without worrying about others' opinions.

I was caught in a conflict. I watched these shows and witnessed these beautiful women around me who took care of themselves and oozed sexuality and sensuality, yet on the flipside I was hearing that if a woman showed up in her beautiful, sexual glory she was no good, she was a slut and looking for attention. I was confused because I was being told to show up dressed to the nines, take care of my appearance, and make sure I looked perfect, yet if I showed up like that, I was going to be considered no good, looking for "trouble" and a slut. Other people's opinions were very important because I was conditioned to live my life by what other people thought of us. Image was EVERYTHING.

As women we are conditioned to suppress our sexuality because it makes us bad; however, everywhere we turn we see images of sexy women in ads, commercials, and social media. We know that sex sells because sex is one of our primal natural instincts. For heaven's sake, sex is how we procreate. Our sexual energy is one of the most creative and one of the highest energy vibrations that we as humans can tap into.

Those ads only confirmed what I was already learning from the women in my life, that sexy was all about image, how you look-ed, and what you wore. Well, there were countless nights when I did my makeup and put a beautiful outfit on and I still felt unattractive. No matter how much I made myself up on the outside if I didn't feel good on the inside, I was never going to feel good. That's far from owning your sexy. The way we look on the outside is often used as an illusion masking our internal, unhealthy landscape.

As I walked this adventure toward my healing, I have come to the realization that our sexy comes from the inside out. Sure, we can put on the sexy clothes and show our bodies like the commercials and movies throw in our face, but the real embodiment of our sexy lies deep within our soul. It comes from our personal qualities. Our character. Our heart. It lives in our feminine divine power that we were conditioned to put a lid on and forget about because the way we women could make it in life was to power-up our masculine energy. Our masculine energy helped us survive, it pushed us to do, to make it through the difficult times. We were told that being in our feminine energy was weak. We were scared into being strong because being vulnerable was an absolute NO; it would lead to getting hurt and taken advantage of.

We were conditioned to wear a mask to hide our true selves.

Hiding our real authentic selves is the most stifling thing we can do. It creates horrible pain within us because we are so out of alignment with who we are, yet we do it all the time because of the rules society and culture imposes on us. Rules that are absolutely self-sabotaging. Society tells us we need to look a certain way to be wanted. Society tells us that we need to act a certain way to be accepted. Society tells us we have to think a certain way to be good. ALL BULLSHIT.

I held on to so many bullshit cultural stories for so long. One of the stories was as a wife and mother I shouldn't leave my young kids and husband for a girls' weekend away or even a girls' night out. I was also entrenched in my masculine energy of doing and productivity. One day my godsister Mimi called and dropped the hammer on me pretty hard. She was getting married in a few months and she wanted me to join her and several other women for her bachelorette party in Cabo, Mexico. She wasn't taking no for an answer. She told me if I continued on my path of focusing only on family and work that I would die just like my mother did. I needed to let loose, get away and have some fun. At that time, in my mind, only bad girls did that. Well, if you know Mimi, you'd understand that I really couldn't say no. Once I said I would go I felt a sense of excitement swell inside of me. I had never gone on a girls' trip like this, not even when I was single. I was inspired to buy myself a new bathing suit, a two-piece which I never would have felt comfortable in the past, and splurged on some new dresses from Victoria's Secret. One of the dresses was a nude crochet mini dress that I still have in my closet to this day because it made me feel so feminine and pretty. For the first time in my life, I felt my feminine energy flow. At that time, I didn't even know it was feminine energy. I was in a state of flow because I gave myself permission to be free. The women I was with were all my friends and sisters, and I was able to laugh, dance, be silly and really own a part of me that I didn't even know existed: The Feminine Divine. That trip was such a catalyst moment for me because I learned it's healthy, not bad, to enjoy yourself independently of your partner and kids, and I was able to flow in the beautiful nurturing energy of the feminine divine.

We all have the masculine and feminine energies within us, and when we embrace both of these God-given energies, we become extraordinary creators. To be in our sensual power we don't have to be confined to look, act, or be any certain way. We get to be who we are at our core, without limitation. When we are our true free selves we emanate a glow, an aura although it isn't something someone can really see, it's an energy of love and joy that radiates outward, making others naturally want to gravitate toward you. I am sure you know that "glow & flow" I am talking about. It's magnetizing. You will become that magnet that glows when you are your true authentic self.

How can we feel sexy and own the magnificent power that our sensuality can create if we suppress it, if we are told we are bad? How can we own our sexy when we are buried in low self-esteem, people-pleasing, lack, and critical self-talk? We can't.

You are valued, you are a goddess,
and don't forget that.

–Jennifer Lopez

My beautiful friend, the fabulousness we have bottled within us as women is powerful and potent beyond belief. I absolutely believe that we underestimate our sexual creative energy and once we learn how to harness it we will attract intimacy, prosperity, and abundance in all areas of our lives. Owning our sensuality will guide us deeper into the core of our spiritual self. Our Soul.

In my humble opinion, owning our sexy isn't about the physical act of sex, it's about our energy! It's about loving who we are. It's about choosing ourselves. It's about being humbly confident. It's about knowing our worth. It's about enjoying life and living in a place of gratitude and joy. That gratitude and joy move us into clarity around our passions and desires.

In healing our trauma and rewriting our stories, we are taking accountability and responsibility for our lives. In healing our trauma and rewriting our stories, we are taking responsibility for our happiness. No one owes us shit. We owe it to ourselves. No one can make us happy; we make ourselves happy. We can't look to the outside for happiness, that happiness comes from within us. We far too often blame our circumstances for our misery when we have choices. Yes, I know sometimes those choices are difficult but, still, we have them. Blaming the world around us for our reality will drain any sexy right out of you and you will only attract unsexy interactions and oftentimes toxic situations.

I believe being in the mud and pain of our ego and insecurities is necessary to really allow us to appreciate the deliciousness of our sensuality. Without experiencing the pain how will we appreciate the ecstasy of standing in our God-given feminine divine energy. The energy that loves, nurtures, attracts, and gives life to those around whoever is lucky enough to feel into the energy of the feminine divine. The challenge arises and we lose our power when we stay in the pain and complaining instead of transmuting it into a passion and zest for life.

Imperfection is beauty, madness is genius and it's
better to be absolutely ridiculous
than absolutely boring.

–Marilyn Monroe

Have you ever noticed that women to whom men are attracted draw the attention of other women as well? They are the ones who walk into the room and light it up with their presence, with their smile, with their charisma. That woman is rarely the most physically attractive woman in the room; she is the woman that feels the most comfortable in her skin. The woman who says what's on her mind and doesn't really care what others are thinking because she knows who she is to her core. She has fun and you can't help but have fun when you are sharing space with her. She is aware of her insecurities and flaws and she recognizes they don't define her. She knows what her gifts are and doesn't use them to manipulate but to influence and inspire. She encourages and uplifts. She gives from a full cup because she wants to not because she wants something in return. She sees you and makes you feel so warm, you never forget how good you feel in her presence. She loves being a woman and embraces the qualities that make her feminine, like her gentle heart. She loves deeply, even though she has had her heart broken many times. She doesn't view other women as competition but as sisters in her tribe who she learns from and creates with.

Although she has her own struggles and challenges, she finds joy in the blessings in her life. Nothing is perfect, yet everything is perfect for her. Even if she was having a bad day she smiled, not because she was fake but because she was grateful. She dances like no one is watching and takes the risk to be in her raw vulnerability and loves with all of her heart.

This woman is flowing in the divine feminine goddess energy, owning her fabulous, sexy self and doesn't even realize it. The woman that is compassionate to herself radiates compassion out. The woman that is loving towards herself radiates love out. The woman that owns her passions and desires radiates that passion out. What we radiate out from our soul comes back to us like a boomerang only multiplied. Embody the qualities that you want to receive from others. Most importantly, she takes accountability for her healing; she knows how to set her boundaries and she walks away from those people and situations that don't serve her. Her discernment is one of her many superpowers. This woman is inside you.

My girlfriends and I love to go out dancing at a local lounge. We love the old-school music, and people-watching, and we laugh our asses off reminiscing about our younger days. We don't even dance on the dance floor, we dance with each other by our table. Just enjoying ourselves, feeling great, and enjoying each other's company without judgment or drama. Just the three us, in our essence doing what we love. Listening to the music and dancing our little hearts out. We were having a blast. The majority of the crowd is our age, forty to fifty-plus, but there is one couple there I love to watch and they're probably in their seventies! I LOVE THEM! They are absolutely owning their sexy!

One of those nights my girlfriend taps me on the shoulder as I am breathing in the beat of the song and asks me if I notice the young girls watching us. I had noticed them. They were two drop-dead gorgeous girls in their twenties, and I noticed that they had been watching us for a while. We both knew that they are watching us because we were in our humble confidence not caring about a thing in the world, laughing, flowing in our feminine divine, and enjoying ourselves and each other. Sexy is releasing inhibitions and being free in the moment to experience connection with yourself and those around you.

I want you to know that no matter what age you are – twenty, thirty, fifty, seventy, eighty – you have every right to own the sexy within you. You are never too old. Age is just a number and you are as old as you feel. I have an eighty-year-old friend and she is a hot mama! She has a red bob with blond highlights and a personality to match and dances Zumba most days of the week. You can't help but be attracted to her fiery fun energy. She embodies sexy.

Sexy comes in all shapes, sizes, and ages. Doesn't matter what you wear or don't wear. Each person is unique and beautiful in their own way. There is no other YOU on this planet. OWN YOU because YOU ARE A BADASS HOT FUCKING MAMA!

Owning your fabulous sexy doesn't mean you never feel insecure. It means you continue to love yourself through those insecurities. Our insecurities are only letting us know where we need deeper healing. Vulnerability is key to intimacy. Intimacy in the relationship with ourselves and with others. We deepen and build trust through vulnerability and emotional intimacy. As we began to share our vulnerability and feel safe, we build trust with ourselves and with others. As you trust others you will feel more confident in your interactions. I know it isn't an easy task to be vulnerable and trust because so many of us have been jaded and I totally get it. Here is another key to the magic of owning your sexy. Realizing that each relationship you enter into, whether platonic or romantic, is teaching you important lessons about yourself. Learn from those experiences. Our relationships uncover our trauma wounds so we can heal them. Relationships are our greatest teachers. Use them as stepping-stones to create healthier interactions and to gather inform-ation about what you do want and don't want in relationships.

Attached or single, we can be in the delightful flow of our sexy because it is a state of mind, an energy vibration, not just a physical act. It is the captivating energy of our lifeforce. It is what attracts to us not only our life partners, lovers, and romantic encounters but it births our children, attracts our abundance, and helps us elevate to reach our greatest potential as human beings. It is an energy that creates that is rarely talked about.

I am here with you to encourage you to shed the layers of self-deprecating critical thoughts and to fall in deep mad love with yourself. There isn't a feeling in the world that is more potent than that feeling of being in love. Fall in love with yourself. Fall in love with your life. Fall in love with the sound of the birds singing first thing in the morning. Fall in love with the sun peeking through the clouds. Fall in love with the feeling your favorite song conjures up in you. Create a deep profound love story with yourself. When you fall in love with yourself the love you desire will overflow into your life in ways you never believed possible. Enjoy being a woman! Have fun with it in any way that feels in alignment for you. There is no right way or no wrong way. Whichever way you choose to embody your sensuality is right for you. Enjoy exploring and discovering the alluring magical Goddess that lives inside of you.

Once you elevate into your humble confidence, own your sexy, embrace your feminine divine and begin having fun, you are going to be addicted. Addicted to the emotions that the fun has elicited through your entire body, mind, and spirit. You will want to stay in that vibrational state. That is one of my favorite emotional states to be in. That is when I feel most connected to my higher self and when I am able to connect with others in a deep, intimate, and meaningful way. Of course, we can't stay in an elevated state of the dopamine rush because it's not realistic; however, we can infuse fun and connection into our lives on a consistent basis. When we feel good, when we are dynamic, when we are connected, when we are in flow, when we are having fun, we keep ourselves in an energy of joy and that energy of joy opens up the doors to greater possibilities. Don't be surprised if once you own your sexy you increase your income, attract incredible new people into your life, and feel a sense of Peace and Freedom.

As you elevate into your Goddess self, your soul will no longer allow you to settle for less than what you deserve in all areas of your life. Especially in all your relationships. You no longer are okay with crumbs in your platonic and romantic relationships. Don't be afraid to voice what you want. If you don't know what that is, take the time to think about it. Just remember that after a lifetime of doing all the giving, it's now time you get ready to receive.

It is unrealistic to believe that one person can meet all of our needs. That's a fairytale story that Disney fed us. Build and nurture the relationships that are fulfilling to you and provide a reciprocity. There are going to be some relationships that meet your need for deep conversation, some relationships that meet your need for fun and silliness, some relationships that meet your need for sex and intimacy, some relationships that meet your need for affection, and some relationships that are there to support you in the darkest times. Be fair to yourself and the people you love. Accept them where they are and appreciate what they bring to the table. If they don't bring anything to the table anymore you can gently choose to make a shift in the relationship or let it go. You get to choose how you want to move forward.

Girl, IT IS TIME!! Unleash the Sexy Bad Ass Goddess that is within you and be unapologetic in asking for what you want! What have you got to lose?

Activity

An amazing activity you can pretty much do anywhere to put you in the flow of your fabulous sexy self is to play your favorite music and DANCE and flirt with life! Dance and flirt your little booty off. Move with the rhythm of the music and just let yourself be and own your sexiness. This will not only get you in the flow it will also give you a boost of dopamine and shift you into a high energy vibration.

Chapter Thirteen

Rise Like the Phoenix!

A strong woman knows she has strength enough for the journey, but a woman of strength knows it is the journey where she will become strong.

–Unknown

I t has been a pleasure and an honor to be here with you. I am so grateful to have your time! Never in a million years did I think that I would be writing a book and sharing the vulnerable moments in my life. I was conditioned to never show vulnerability, that to do so was weak and tarnished the perfect image we were supposed to maintain. I learned early on how to wear many different masks depending on the audience and situation. To say it's been a gift to share my authenticity and views with you is an understatement. Sharing has helped me dive deeper into my own healing and embrace even more peace and freedom from the constraints society puts on us.

I believe in progress, not perfection, and I believe that everything is perfect in the moment. As long as we are breathing there will be more for us to learn and there will be deeper levels of expansion for us to experience. I am not going to front and tell you this has been an easy journey. It has been very challenging at times, but the flipside of the coin is it has been so exhilarating, fun, joyous, and connected. You need to have grit, resilience, and determination to move from fucked up to fabulous. (FYI: none of us are truly fucked up – we are all on our own journey towards fabulous, regardless of where we start.) There are going to be days, probably many of them, when you just feel like giving up and falling into easier, comfortable habits. I am here to remind you to resist that temptation, for those comfortable habits are what will keep you entangled in the web of mediocrity and playing small.

You are the magic, own that shit!

–Unknown

Even at the young age of ten I was a tough little cookie. One of my favorite movies series was Rocky, and I recorded the soundtrack off the radio with my cassette player (yes, I am dating myself) and listened to "Eye of the Tiger" and "Gonna Fly Now" over and over. The movies and those songs *pumped me the fuck up*! Whenever I felt defeated and depressed, I would play them and imagine Rocky, bloody and bruised, rising off the floor, and my ass would jump up and do the same. Even today when I hit a wall, I turn on the Rocky songs and visualize him. My saying is, "FUCK THAT, I AM NOT GOING DOWN!"

Fall down seven times stand up eight.

–Japanese proverb

This life, my friend, is yours to author! The information I have provided in this book isn't the end all, be all. It is, however, what has helped me level-up and expand. It helped me unlearn the beliefs society handed me and go against the status quo, and I believe it will help you do the same. Remember, the status quo worked to benefit those who created it. Now, as we evolve as a collective and especially as women, it doesn't have to be that way.

Rome wasn't built in a day and no one climbs Mt. Everest in a day. Great wins require small, daily victories, so it is your commitment and consistency each day that will propel you to success. You are planting the seeds of your garden so that one day, perhaps sooner than you think, you'll just have to walk in and pick the fruit from the trees.

One day I was standing at the sink, washing dishes and feeling overwhelmed as I thought of everything else I needed to get done. I was still in my core story of having to do more and more to receive. Then, as I stared at a lemon tree in my backyard, a light bulb came on in my head. The tree was overflowing with lemons, so many that they were falling off the tree onto the dirt below. I realized in that moment that I had planted many seeds in my garden of life and all I had to do now was nurture the garden and the fruits would grow in abundance with little effort. It took almost ten years for that lemon tree to provide such abundance. What I realized was that our efforts compound and create the harvest – our commitment and consistent action are the soil and the water. I was guided to make some time and pick the lemons off the tree. A few mornings later I went out during a crisp misty morning and I started picking the lemons off the tree one by one. As I picked each lemon, I took a deep breath in and honored all of the hard work and effort I had put into my life. Raising my family, building a business, healing and diminishing my childhood trauma wounds, releasing old stories and creating new empowering ones, nurturing both easy and challenging relationships, and putting a tremendous amount of effort into my own growth and expansion.

Picking the lemons off the tree that morning was such a beautiful spiritual experience for me. Since then, I have released even more of my core story of doing to receive, and these days the abundance I receive comes with little effort because of the seeds I planted in my lifetime. I promise you, the effort you put in today that seems so painstaking is absolutely worth it; remember, my friend, you get out of life what you put into it.

If you really want something you will find a way. If you really don't you will find an excuse.

–Unknown

Like many truths, the above quote seems so simple when it's really not. While it is absolutely necessary to vent, bitch, and talk things out (this serves to process your feelings and move negative thoughts and energy out of your mind and body), we often amplify our stress by complaining and ruminating on the shit that isn't working for us for far too long. As you begin your dance toward fabulous, I challenge you to start to get curious when you get stressed. Our stress triggers are messages from our soul on where we need to do the healing work. We are rarely responding to the present moment, but a past experience that wounded us and led to the creation of a fucked-up story around it. When we know our worth and own our fabulousness, the intensity of our triggers will start to diminish. When we get curious and have awareness of why we are acting the way we do, it helps us heal our wounds and take our power back. Just a small nugget of wisdom I would like you to be aware of: we are all children in adult bodies, responding from the wounded child that is within us. As we heal those wounds, we graduate to the next grade level of consciousness and freedom.

Think like a queen. A queen is not afraid to fail.
Failure is another stepping-stone to greatness.

– Oprah Winfrey

As you continue on your adventure to level-up, keep in mind the sheer volume of information out there that can help you reach your greatest potential. Allow yourself the time to integrate the information that resonates with you, be it in this book or elsewhere. This process takes a lifetime, and our minds and spirit can only take in and manage so much information at a time. Just like it took time to create your current habits, give yourself time to integrate your new empowering habits. Be gentle with yourself and allow yourself to fall off the wagon, knowing that is normal. All you need to do is just get back on the next day or the day after. Even if you've fallen off for months you can get back on; just ask yourself, how falling off is benefiting you (i.e., the safety of returning to your comfort zone). Then, ask yourself how it will benefit you to get back on the good habit train. You'll find your desired outcome will far outweigh your present circumstances.

Being in control is such a big factor for so many of us. I totally get it. Our need to control creates a sense of safety for us. As a recovering control freak, I can tell you that when we make an effort to control circumstances that are out of our control, or try to control others and get them to do what we want them to, we are actually creating resistance and will never get what we want. As you process the information in this book and begin to integrate the lessons, you will realize that control is based in fear. Creating new stories will allow you to begin releasing that dense energy of fear and open yourself up to remarkable opportunities that feel like miracles.

Please remember that our outer world is a reflection of how we feel inside of ourselves. If you are continuously attracting shit you don't like, it's time to stop and ask yourself where you are a match to this situation. My life used to be drama-filled; today, it is very rare that I experience any drama. The love that I have cultivated for myself broadcasts out to the world, resulting in a majority of my harmonious, loving experiences. In those instances when they are not, I set a boundary, choose me, speak my peace, or walk away. This is because I've learned to recognize that I'm out of alignment within myself and it's time to make a shift. Again, it isn't right or wrong it's just an awareness to get back on track.

Although self-discovery and expansion is a lifelong process, I promise that you will immediately begin to benefit, even from the little steps you take. One thing I have struggled with, as well as so many of my colleagues and clients, is that we cannot change other people, only ourselves. As you begin to elevate, you may no longer be a vibrational match with the people in your life. You will start to notice that you don't have as much in common as you used to. You may even find yourself in conflicts with the people you love, that they drain your energy. You are going to want to bring them with you as you elevate to incredible new heights. Your heart will break when you realize they aren't ready for the next steps, even though you see their light and their incredible potential. My friend, they need to see it for themselves. Do not try to change them or give them advice if they don't want it; instead, know that by elevating your life you are planting a seed for them and setting the example of what is possible for them. You are influencing the world around you and you won't even realize it! Keep in mind that when the student is ready the teacher will appear. Each person needs to be ready. We can't push our beliefs onto them.

It isn't fair to them or to us.

There have been weeks and months where I felt like things weren't happening fast enough for me and I grew tired of being committed and consistent to my healthy habits. In those moments I remembered the movie *The Shawshank Redemption*. The main character Andy Dufresne is sentenced to life in prison for a crime he didn't commit. Determined to get out, he makes a rock hammer and starts picking at the wall in his cell each night when the other inmates are asleep. Each day, he hides the hole he is making with a poster. For nineteen years, he picks at the wall little by little until one day he can fit through the hole. He escapes prison and goes to live the rest of his life on the beach. Call me crazy, but I always think back to the wall when I want to give up. I keep moving forward, realizing that the committed intention and effort will bring incredible benefits in all areas of my life.

You wouldn't be reading this book if you didn't have a vision or a dream buried deep inside you. Due to life's circumstances, you may have forgotten about that dream. Through the negative messages that society and the world at large whispers to us, you have been discouraged to believe that your dream is even possible. *It is possible.* Just like it was possible for Andy to escape from prison, it is absolutely possible for you to escape the prison of your mind to live the life you dream of. Fabulous isn't just for others, it is for you too! It is your choice! You get to choose how you want to write your story from here. Now that you know what is possible, your soul won't allow you to stay in the mediocre. We assign the meaning to the situations in our lives. You may have been living in the victim role without even realizing it. This likely stems from childhood, when you learned to assign victim mentality meaning to the situations as a way to appease your ego. The child in you that needed the attention, needed to feel safe.

Sister are you ready?! It is time to rise into your fabulous. You have all the power within you to design the life you desire. After all, you are badass woman who has already accomplished a shit ton. You care for those around you, even when you don't feel like getting up. Many of you have raised families single-handedly, and/or made it through challenging-as-fuck toxic relationships and managed exhausting situations. You are the caretakers of your family and friends. Now it's all about YOU! You didn't come into this lifetime to play small, and you don't need to do so to make others feel better. Lisa Nicholas said, "It is our greatest fear to be fabulous." We worry about what others will say. They may think we are stuck up. We don't want to leave anyone behind. Girl, when you step it up and rise you aren't leaving anyone behind. You are becoming a role model for what they can aspire to be. When we get triggered by another person's success that's really our higher self, making us uncomfortable and nudging us toward the vision of what is possible for us. I want you to take this in as TRUTH, no one who is more successful than you is going to be hating on you. Don't take the haters personally.

It is your God-given right to elevate to the frequency of un-limited abundance and fabulousness! You don't have to earn it or deserve it to claim it. It is already yours. The only thing holding you back from claiming the next level of prosperity is you. There is no judgment or shame in this, I am just bringing it to your attention.

You get to choose today and every day. We are not going to bat a hundred every day, and we don't need to. It's the small choices we make each and every day that move us toward the magic. It's the small actions we take for granted that compound and give us the big bang. I didn't get to where I am overnight. It was the tiny consistent and committed baby steps. Also, make sure to throw in some fun in there as well. There are many days when I enjoy the fuck out of dirty martinis, eat decadent, delicious meals, skip work to play, binge Netflix shows, and dance until two a.m. We all need fun! It is necessary for our soul and puts us in a tantalizing incredible flow that opens us up to marvelous possibilities.

If your actions create a legacy that inspires others to dream more, learn more, do more and become more, then you are an excellent leader.

–Dolly Parton

Recognize that all the shit you have been through – the betrayals, the gaslighting, the broken hearts, the noes, the rejections (actually, those weren't really rejections, it was God redirecting you! Girl, believe me, you were being saved from some BULL-SHIT!) – were all making you wiser. Could they have also made you bitter? Fo' sho'. But guess what, girl? It is time to surrender that bitterness because the big leagues are ready and waiting for you.

You've put so much effort into others. You have witnessed others thrive and succeed from the support and nurturing you have provided. Now it's your turn! Time to put the energy that you put into everyone else into you.

No, girl, it's not selfish at all. It's self-love. We can no longer give from an empty cup like much of the generations before us did. It benefits no one. And who wants to drink from a cup full of resentment and bitterness anyway? That's salty, and the people you want to bring closer to you will only run away because our energy speaks louder than our words or actions. Our faces wear our emotions. You know that. You can feel it when someone is unauthentic and doing something because they want something in return. That's manipulative and ratchet, so don't be that person.

The words that have poured onto these pages come directly from my heart. They are words based on my experiences and on my lifestyle practices. My experiences and words may not resonate with everyone and that's okay because *I* am not for everyone. My passion is to be an example to others of what is possible. Living in my own prison of my mind for so long and then experiencing the incredible freedom on the other side is what inspired me to become vulnerable and put myself out there. I want everyone to live a life that they want to wake up to each morning, not run away from. A life that brings them joy, laughter, connection, and magical miracles. Our lives can absolutely be extraordinary even when the collective around us is in chaos. I want you to know that the more of us that step into our extraordinary the more we help ease that chaos, and heal the generations before us and ahead of us.

Even when living our fabulous life, we are going to experience messy moments. This is life, so don't be hard on yourself when shit doesn't go your way. Know that you can be fabulous and navigate the messy at the same time. That's real talk.

Be like the Phoenix and continue to rise and reinvent yourself through each season of your life. What you want today may not be what you want tomorrow and that's okay. You get to design your life the way you want every step of the way. Be kind to yourself and allow yourself space to be flexible and fluid on this dazzling adventure called life.

Now, I dare you to LIVE and go from Fucked UP to FAB-ULOUS!

I LOVE YOU!

Epilogue

Difficult roads often lead to
beautiful destinations.

—**Melchor** Lim

The following words are the rawest and most vulnerable that I have shared to date. They are the most vulnerable, not only because they involve me but my family as well. I have always made an effort to respect their privacy as much as possible; however, I don't believe I would have felt true to myself if I didn't share this with you. I share the following words with the utmost respect and love, and with the permission of Mike and our sons, for which I am eternally grateful.

On July 5, 2022, I submitted the draft of this manuscript to my publisher. It was such an exhilarating moment. I had never even imagined writing a book, yet there I was, about to share, on a much larger scale than ever before, how I made a one-eighty-degree, major transformation that included breaking deep generational patterns. The date itself was also significant, as I had just spent a fabulous Fourth of July weekend with friends and family. It was also seven months into an epic "post-pandemic" year of incredible vacations, fun, and attracting abundance with more ease and grace than ever before.

The decades of healing; the difficult, deep-dive work into my limiting beliefs, childhood wounds and self-sabotaging patterns; and my recent, intuitively-led experiment to work even less and play even more now made sense. It had all been leading me to this moment.

On July 19, while wrapping up my day at the office, I received a phone call from my doctor with the results of a recent biopsy of two growths sitting on my thyroid. She informed me that they were indeed cancerous, requiring a complete thyroidectomy. She assured me that all would be well; I would just need to be on thyroid hormone pills for the rest of my life. My reaction: WTF, REALLY?! I was annoyed as FUCK! I had way too many things planned ahead to be slowed down, even if only for a few months. (And, yes, I was also very grateful that it was a treatable type of cancer and that it was caught early – but, again, WTF!)

In my heart I had NO DOUBT that I would be fine. I was more concerned about interrupting the life that I had worked so hard to create. I was in one of the best places ever – emotionally, mentally, physically, and financially – and this was the last thing I wanted to deal with. I wanted to continue on the trajectory of travel, fun, and connection. Now, to be real, a few months earlier, I had an intuitive feeling that I would be dealing with a cancer diagnosis, but I thought I was just imagining things and kept moving. Our higher self ALWAYS knows. Make sure to listen!

I went home and told Mike and the boys the news, assuring them that I would be fine and they need not worry. I chose not to share this with anyone in the family, as we had several important celebrations on the horizon and I didn't want to worry or scare anyone. However, I did choose a very small circle, including my mentors, to share with for support during my seven-week healing journey leading up to the surgery.

Though the prognosis was good, it was still overwhelming, and I needed a few days to process it. When I did call my naturopath to inform her of the situation, I was a bit taken aback by her reaction. Actually, "floored" is a better description of how I felt. She told me I would never be the same again, that my health would decline from here, and I would experience complications. My first thought was, *Really? Do you know who the fuck you are talking to?! People who are diagnosed with stage-4 cancer survive and even heal. I have a strong mindset I have no doubt that I will emerge from this situation in optimal health.* My second thought was, Thank God I had done all this work on mindset and how it had prepared me for this experience. If I hadn't, and I was still living as I had in the past, her words could have really damaged me. I could have ruminated on them and gone down a deep, black, ugly hole.

I then remembered a naturopath that I had gone to years earlier, with great results, so I called him. I told him the situation and let him know I wanted to start my healing process even before the surgery. He agreed it would be a good idea, and I scheduled an appointment a few days later.

In the days that followed, I found myself increasingly irritated with the situation. This was such a pain in my ass! I wanted to continue to focus on my fun social calendar, booking amazing guests on my podcast, meeting with my coaching clients, supporting my staffing clients and candidates, and connecting with the people I love. I just wanted to enjoy my year of BEING! It was as if the Universe was saying, *Ya, bitch, that's what you think. I have a way different plan for you.* Now I had to be real with myself and ask, *How the fuck and why the fuck did I manifest this shit?* I was not blaming myself in any way, shape, or form because fucked-up shit does happen, but I also know that the body keeps score. It wasn't a coincidence that I received the annoying news just two weeks after I poured my heart out in a book about how I went from fucked up to fabulous!

It was a Monday morning when I went to meet with my naturopath. Mondays are typically my busiest day, and that was the last place I wanted to be. I was also exhausted because it had been a draining weekend between my social commitments and processing the diagnosis. The doctor asked how I was doing, and I told him that I had really been great. And I was a very different woman from the one he had seen almost a decade earlier.

"That's great, Grace, but this situation means you have life changes to make."

"I totally get it," I said, "I have made so many life changes."

Then came the questions: "Do you exercise?"

"Yes, every day."

"Do you eat well?"

"Yup, I am on top of my food choices."

"Get out in nature?"

"Yup. Since the pandemic, at least two of my workouts a week are outside."

"Do you meditate?"

"Again, every day. I even have professional coaches that I meet with twice a month. I am on top of my shit."

Then he asked me the question: "What is your homelife like?'"

I started going on about how great Mike and the boys are, how other than never picking up after themselves they were really a joy, and we had fun with them. I told him how I had created Disneyland at home, and we had a privileged, overall, really good life…

Then, suddenly, I had an awareness, and the emotions in my chest started to swell. My stomach turned and the floodgates opened. Through my tears and the pain in my chest, I finally managed to get the words out: "My husband is an alcoholic!" The crying continued, and my body felt heavy and ached terribly.

"Grace," he said, "how long have you been picking up the pieces?"

"For twenty-seven years, and I am tired!"

I went home that afternoon feeling both relieved and depleted. I felt relief because although I'd known for years that alcohol was a huge factor in the challenges I experienced in my marriage, I had never, until that moment, seen the situation for what it was. I had really struggled with Mike for many years and in many ways; however, I'd learned to focus on the good things in the relationship. He was home every night, he loved coaching the boys in their sports, he was successful in his career, he respected me, and he valued my drive and ambition.

When we were first married, my mom would always tell me, in her Middle Eastern accent, "Grace, Mike … he drinks A LOT." I didn't really think anything of it. We were in our twenties, and that's what you do. You drink and party and have fun.

There were challenges between us even in the early days, but I didn't realize that they were due to the alcoholism. Instead, I internalized those challenges and made them about me. I wasn't good enough. He didn't find me attractive. He wasn't interested in me. So what did I do? I tried harder. I made sure I was in the best physical shape. I made sure I took care of myself (because, as mentioned earlier, I'd heard that he would leave me when I got old, fat, and ugly). I made sure the house was perfect, that dinner was always cooked, and that I made plenty of money so he didn't have to stress. I always had fun plans for us, and, as the doctor pointed out, I always picked up the pieces when the irresponsibility that resulted from his drinking kicked in. I take accountability for the enabling and the lack of boundary-setting. Part of my behavior was unconscious; I was just doing what I thought I had to do: keep everything afloat and "perfect" at all costs. You don't know what you don't know until you know it. I needed my family to stay grounded and organized, and I needed my boys to feel safe in their environment. Mike loved his life, and he always told me how happy he was, and I was "the best," but there was always something coming between us, and that something was alcohol. I was settling for crumbs and didn't even realize it. I was too busy in survival mode when the kids were young, and I was dealing with so much – sick parents, a busy business, and the continuous family drama.

I talked and talked and pleaded for change; however, it's not that easy. Alcoholism is a real struggle. The term "high-functioning alcoholic" is such bullshit. You typically just function at your bare minimum. As the years progressed, I just told myself that no relationship is perfect and accepted mine for what it was. I was grateful that I wasn't experiencing the abuse other women in my life had. Plus, my life really was Disneyland compared to the damaging and devastating abuse I myself had endured as a child and young adult from those who were supposed to protect me and make me feel safe. At least I felt protected and safe in the home we had created together.

I do remember one time, in the early years, going to my father and saying, "Dad, something is off at home with Mike."

"Does he beat you?" Dad asked.

"No."

"Does he cheat on you?"

"No, not that I know of."

"Does he swear at you? No? So what's the problem?"

As I look back on that conversation now, it makes me sad. As women we are so used to giving so much of ourselves and receiving so little back. We deserve so much more than crumbs. We deserve the whole loaf.

As the relationship progressed, and I didn't see any changes, I started on my own healing journey. I had nothing left to give, and it was time to give to myself. I learned that I could only change myself and started focusing on doing that. I pulled my energy back from the relationship with Mike and directed it instead toward the relationship between myself and God. I stopped trying to control something I had no control over. I accepted Mike where he was on his journey and focused on the good qualities like I had learned in my high-level coaching classes. It started to work well. At that point, the boys were grown, and we had the opportunity to start traveling all over and really enjoying ourselves. We lived, and still live, a really incredible, privileged life. We were good friends who had lots of fun together, and who wouldn't want that in a marriage? All that fun and travel were great distractions from the underlying problem.

Little did I realize that, unconsciously, I felt suffocated and trapped. I wasn't being seen, heard, or acknowledged, and my basic needs weren't being met in what was supposed to be one of the most important relationships in my life. Now I understood why the nodules had grown on my thyroid. The thyroid sits on our throat. Our throat is where we express ourselves. In my experience as a child and now as a woman, the people closest to me rarely, if ever, saw me, heard me, or acknowledged me. When I expressed myself, both as a child and as a woman, I was "shot down," was dismissed, or called "too sensitive" or "crazy." I was gaslighted. My soul needed to be heard, seen, and acknowledged, and I needed my basic needs to be met. What was once working because I didn't know any better no longer was.

The two weeks that followed my realization in the naturopath's office were profoundly difficult. It wasn't admitting the truth to the naturopath that was so difficult and painful; it was admitting the truth to myself. I had to also admit that the last few years had become increasingly challenging. I'd thought it was because of the pandemic and having to modify our lives. Although that was part of the challenge, the real issue was that I was having a harder and harder time navigating the alcoholism, especially since I had done so much of my own healing and had a much higher level of awareness of what is really happening. I am a fairly quiet person; I accept things for what they are, and we live a quiet, harmonious life. Well – not during those two weeks! I exploded several times at home in a way I never had before. I needed to let out the years of resentment and grief I didn't even realize I had out of my body. As I stated earlier in the book, when we internalize our pain, it manifests physically. Again, I am not blaming myself – I am just aware of our mind, body, spirit connection. Okay, now back to my anger and exploding. Girl, let me tell you, that shit was so damn healing! I never like to hurt anyone's feelings, and I am always careful with what I say but, damn, there are times you just need to be real as fuck with people, *especially* if you care about them. I swear, during those two weeks, I felt like a character out of *The Exorcist!*

As a result of my expressing my anger in this new (and loud) way, Mike acknowledged his alcoholism and the behavior stemming from it, which really helped validate me and made me feel like I wasn't crazy. My boys also validated my feelings and expressed their own challenges with the situation. In that moment, I felt an empowerment and relief I hadn't felt before. I was able to exhale. I had expressed myself and was heard instead of being dismissed or feeling like I was expecting too much. Now I was ready to focus on myself and prepare for my surgery a little over a month away.

Over the next five weeks, I met with my mentors several times to process the resentment and grief that had come up. I continued my regular routine of meditation, working out, and being in nature. It was still summertime, so I enjoyed lots of music in the park and fun activities with friends and family. In the days before my surgery, I felt complete. I felt strong and empowered. I was asked if I was afraid. Of course, I had fearful thoughts – that is normal; however, I never ruminated on them. I had this feeling of absolute trust. I knew without a doubt that God had my back, like He always does. It was an amazing feeling I had never felt before. The night before my surgery, I sat on my bed and cried. I cried because I felt that all the challenging experiences I'd faced and all of the deep healing work I'd done were preparing me for the next chapter of my life. I felt like my body had purged so much in the years prior, and this was the final purge of the pain that was secretly hidden there. I do believe writing my book brought so much more to the surface that I wasn't even aware of to be purged. It was like I was experiencing another metamorphosis, like the caterpillar that goes into a cocoon and emerges a beautiful butterfly.

As long as we are alive and breathing, we are going to face challenges and adversities, no matter how much healing we have experienced. I truly believe that if I hadn't committed to the principles I have shared in this book, my life and diagnosis would look very different. Frankly, I know I would be a hot damn mess right now instead of feeling empowered and strong.

This experience has also helped me dive deeper into the practices I have shared. I surrender to the perfect pictures that still pop up in my mind and remind myself that it's about progress, not perfection. I accept that no matter what I do, I can't change another person; they need to be ready for that change. I recognize that one of the most difficult concepts to practice is accepting people and honoring where they are on their journey. I understand that I have choices, and I know what is best for me. I trust myself, my intuition, and the process. I now realize that we attract our partners based on our childhood traumas and triggers. I am very grateful that we were able to create a beautiful family and life together, despite the challenges. Mike has been one of my greatest teachers.

As part of my pre-surgery healing, I was guided to pick up *The Power of Now* by Eckhart Tolle. His words resonated with me and helped me make sense of my experience. He writes that all relationships, particularly romantic ones, are deeply flawed and dysfunctional. Our relationships trigger our insecurities, trauma, and pain. It is necessary for each of us to address our own shit first to create truly healthy partnerships. Typically, there is one partner who is open to doing the work and another partner who just isn't ready. We are each the teacher and the student in this schoolyard called life. We must not take other people's actions personally. Remember, people with whom we are in relationships can only meet us at the level of consciousness that they can meet themselves. They can only love us to the level that they are able to love themselves. They can only give us to the point they can give themselves. No one can give to us if their own well is dry. Now, are there healthy relationships in which both people commit to the work? Absolutely.

Life ebbs and flows and is an exploration of self-discovery. It is up to us if we choose to stay entrenched in our suffering and struggle or explore new creative ways of living in freedom and peace.

I must learn to give those I love the right to make their own mistakes and recognize them as theirs alone.

–Al-Anon

Alcoholism affects so many more individuals and families than we realize – and in so many different ways. The person doesn't have to come home drunk throwing up every night in a violent rage to impact the family dynamic. I am not making this about right or wrong; it just is. Ultimately, we each get to choose how we want to navigate our relationships. What might be right for one person may not be right for another. What is right for one family may not be right for another. There is support if we choose. If you are struggling with a loved one who is an alcoholic, I would recommend reaching out to a friend, visiting an Al-Anon meeting, or even reaching out to me. I am here to support you. The one thing I don't recommend is continuing to deny there is a problem.

We live in a this-AND-that world, not a this-OR-that world. We can navigate the messy and live fabulous at the same time. We can be in pain and experience joyful moments. We can set boundaries with a loved one and still be there to support them. We can be grateful and acknowledge the areas of our life that we desire more and better from.

Although I am still in the post-surgery healing phase, I do feel like an absolutely different person. I feel like I have shed the previous decades of my life from my body and I am embarking on an entirely new chapter of life – "The Second Act," as I like to call it. It feels exciting and exhilarating. I feel an even greater freedom than I ever have before. It is so true what they say that the deeper the healing, the more vulnerable we get; the harder conversations we have, the greater the freedom and joy on the other side. It's like the beautiful purple onion – there is just layer and layer of beauty to be pulled back, beauty we aren't even aware is there. It lies in contrast to the fucked-up shit. I know there are many lessons and opportunities for me in this experience. As of right now, I am allowing myself to stay present to the process. I trust that all will unfold exactly the way it is meant to for the greatest and highest good of all involved.

I knew I was a resilient, fierce, strong person; however, this experience has really allowed me to own my resilience, fierceness, and strength. I am no doubt the Phoenix rising through the ashes once again into an even more fabulous wiser version of myself.

Thank you for being open to hear what was on my heart. Stay fabulous and continue to Rise!

I love you and appreciate you.

Grace

October 17th, 2022

Acknowledgments

There are countless people I would like to thank for their love, support, and encouragement throughout my journey. I am so blessed with, and beyond grateful for, incredible family, friends, communities, and circles and I know I couldn't have written this book without the meaningful connections, deep conversations, and experiences that God has gifted me through these real-life angels. You know who you are. **I LOVE YOU ALL SO MUCH!**

To my husband, Mike, thank you for your unconditional love, friendship, and for being my greatest cheerleader. I love you.

To my sons, Raymond and Rami, you give me life! You are incredible souls and there has been no greater accomplishment than raising you. I am SO Excited to see what you create! And thank you for making me laugh every day.

To my assistant and right hand, Allison Tsukamoto and to our Dare to Achieve and Stansbury Staffing Team. Thank you SO much for your support! I couldn't do all I do without you. I love and appreciate you all.

To Jalil Nazzal, thank you so much for giving us the saying "Can I Live." May we all laugh and be as joyous and free as you are each day.

To Wardena, thank you for countless soulful conversations. Words can't even express the gratitude I feel for you, and I am excited to continue co-creating fabulous. Love you to the moon and back.

To Sunny Dawn Johnson, my mentor, you had me at HELLO, girl. Thank you so much for all you do for this world. You are a true angel. You taught me how to choose me while continuing to be kind, loving, authentic, and generous.

To Shanda Trofe, my publisher, for without you this book would have not been possible. You held my hand every step of the way and encouraged me. You actually made me believe that I am a writer!

To Melissa Kim Corter, my mentor who really helped me shift some major limiting beliefs while writing this book. Thank you for holding space for me while I unraveled deep-seated generational trauma. You are a shining light in the darkness for so many.

Most importantly, to GOD, for all the incredible blessings You gift me each and every day. You never fail me and continuously guide me to higher levels of clarity, wisdom, and experiences.

About the Author

Grace Redman is a success coach and entrepreneur who has owned and managed one of the most successful staffing firms in the Bay Area for over twenty years. She is also a success coach who uses a wide variety of methods and tools to help ambitious, heart-centered women elevate their confidence, optimize their talents, and increase their prosperity mindset to push past mediocrity and manifest their dreams.

Grace is no stranger to adversities, from which she gained the wisdom and strength to achieve personal and professional success. Intuitive, down to earth, and fun, she takes a realistic approach to coaching, based on her belief that we can create soul-centered, fabulous, fulfilling lives and businesses without sacrificing ourselves or our relationships.

Grace loves celebrating and highlighting the heroes in her own backyard. As host of the podcast *Real Talk with Grace Redman*, she chats with amazing people from her circles and communities who have overcome challenges to manifest incredible lives. She is also the co-author of several books, including, *365 Days of Self Love*, *Kindness Crusader*, *The Grateful Soul*, *The Wild Woman's Book of Shadows*, and *Manifestations*.

If you are interested in connecting with Grace or inquiring about her one-on-one coaching sessions, visit her at **www.daretoacieve.com**

You can also connect with her below:

www.facebook.com/graceredmandaretoachieve

www.instagram.com/gracesredman

If you enjoyed this book, please feel free to leave a review on Amazon.

CPSIA information can be obtained
at www.ICGtesting.com
Printed in the USA
LVHW011912111222
735004LV00005B/590

9 798986 850719